Health - Remedies   5.75

MW01017011

10-03

Beyond
Turmoil

Beyond Turmoil

A Guide to Renewal
Through Deep Personal Change

by Alice Mack, Ed.D.

Connexions Unlimited
Tucson, Arizona

© 1992 by Alice H. Mack, Ed.D.

Published by
Connexions Unlimited
7344 North Oracle Road, Suite 194
Tucson, AZ 85704
Printed in U.S.A.
9 8 7 6 5 4 3 2 1

Book production by
Summerlin Publishing Group
P.O. Box 32012, Tucson, Arizona 85751-2012

The Dane Rudhyar quotation from *Culture, Crisis and Creativity* (1977), in the front of this book is used with permission from The Theosophical Publishing House, Wheaton, Illinois.

Publisher's Cataloging in Publication
(Prepared by Quality Books Inc.)

Mack, Alice H., 1943-
      Beyond turmoil : a guide to renewal through deep personal change
/ Alice H. Mack.
      p. cm.
      Includes bibliographical references.
      ISBN 0-9632450-7-4

      1. Change (Psychology) 2. Climacteric--Psychological aspects.
3. Self-perception. 4. Self-actualization (Psychology) I.
Title. II. Title: A guide to renewal through deep personal change.

BF637.C4M3 1992   116
                              QBI92-315

Many unmentioned people provided the stories from which the incidents in this book were constructed. Actual names, locations and details, however, have been liberally altered while retaining the essence of their experience. Some portraits represent composites.

Contents

With thanks to Brian Brooks and Katherine Rothrock-Illig,
midwives to my journey.

Mankind is indeed facing a crisis similar to the "change of life" experienced by individual men and women in their forties and fifties. It is a biological and psychological turning point. Both the individual person and the organizational character of human society are confronted with radical change. This change has a truly planetary character. It implies the need for fundamental reorientation of consciousness and a repolarization of human activity; and the central problem is a reevaluation of the meaning and function of individuality. The *feeling of being I-myself* must be given a new meaning.

Dane Rudhyar, *Culture, Crisis and Creativity*

Acknowledgments

Special thanks to Brian Brooks, a gifted therapist, for helping me access and heal the deepest reaches. Katherine Rothrock-Illig, therapist-teacher, nurtured the integration phase. Today she supplies loving wisdom and helps keep me balanced. Those who shared special strength along the way include Suzanne Losee, Nancy and Roger Elsinger, Kyle Reno, Barbara Smith, Dick Davies, Peggy Jones, Don Rott, Mary Jo McCoy, Maggi Hanson, Lenore Bright, Mary Lou Burum, Linda Popov, Chuck Ragland, Lucille Bader, Sherry Johnson, Brad Williams, Linda Drake, David Van Wyck and Jerry Willenbring.

Bob Joanis, compassionate lawyer and family friend, made a real difference during some dark times. Gordon Dveirin and John Brennan propelled me to the writing, plus John helped name the book and supported the new business. Maurice Simons continually cheered me on during the book's crystallization and was tireless about opening doors. Ken Graun provided wonderful graphics, laughter and the cover concept. Michael Snell helped me evolve a writing style. Donald Marrs, Paige Reynolds and Stuart Gellman encouraged the publishing venture through their example and sound advice. Dan Gilmore lent marketing savvy to both book and business. Randy Summerlin and the Summerlin Publishing Group painstakingly produced a quality volume in record time.

People such as Elisabeth Kubler-Ross, Peter Caddy and Brugh Joy enlightened me with their public lectures as well as their personal presence. Years ago Larry Wilson inspired me to pursue knowledge of human growth and its practical applications.

Special thanks to Sharon Greer for her wonderful pencil sketch on the back cover that captures my essence. Nora Holstein supplied a legacy of the feminine virtues through her artful cooking, crochet and caring for others. Finally, the book would never have been completed without Elizabeth Sherburne Ross, my colleague, beloved friend and a flesh and blood guardian angel. Her support and love made the essential difference.

Introduction

Looking backwards, I now see that the inner journey that so drastically altered my life began over a decade ago. Initially I had no idea that a deep transition was underway. During those early years, there was restless self-questioning. Who was I? What did I really want? Was this all there was to life? By day I pursued my career as an organization development consultant, management trainer and part-time college teacher. By night or on weekends, if I wasn't being a workaholic, I lived a secret existence. Episodes included reckless romantic or sexual liaisons, sometimes drinking to excess and swinging between hope and despair.

By the time I turned 40, the symptoms of inner grief and "unfinished business" were deepening. "Unfinished business" means the emotional, often hidden baggage about childhood that most of us carry into adulthood. To alleviate my distress, I undertook three years of rigorous therapy. This work was a follow-up to a year of group therapy where I dealt with a disastrous personal relationship.

The therapist I chose, a practitioner of Jin Shin Jyutsu, used gentle touch on the acupressure points of my body to sense blockages or armoring. As the energy began to move, I experienced the release of stored memories and pain. Months of startling insights followed. Some were related to growing up in an alcoholic family; others went beyond the personal and made little rational sense. Stubborn internal conflicts surfaced regularly as did deep-rooted emotional and physical pain. The content for our sessions came from the internal material, my consulting clients, personal relationships and a family business crisis that forced me to reexamine the dynamics in that family.

During the middle phase of this process, the work was so demanding that I had little energy for anything else. There was no desire initially to understand what was happening. My only interest was to release the pain and get through this; otherwise I was bewildered by the experience. My graduate education had been heavily based in psychology, but I knew of nothing that could explain the flashbacks and sensations that emerged during or after therapy sessions. Having no guide, it was all I could do to find the strength to keep going.

To help myself cope, I made lengthy journal entries after each therapy session and often in between. Friends were another source of inspiration; often they would describe incidents or patterns that rang true for me as well. Soon it became obvious that many of us were stumbling through a new kind of inner frontier. We proceeded with varying degrees of resiliency and success. The means we used, from workshops to therapy, study groups, prayer and treatment centers, ranged the full spectrum.

By the mid-1980s I started to read again, searching for the understanding to explain this internal growth. Having weathered the darkest hours, it clearly stood as the most important "work" I'd ever done. True mental health and a renewed zest for life now beckoned.

As my outlook brightened, however, the frustration with consulting grew. Now I could see more clearly that the root cause of organization problems lay in persons. Our unconscious beliefs and conflicts create behavior that is often highly dysfunctional. Thus, the tools I was trained to use, such as organization diagnosis and feedback, conflict resolution, team-building and participatory planning seemed to be Band-Aids. Such strategies merely scratched the surface. By now I could see that only *deep personal change,* of the type that I and my friends had undertaken, would make a difference in changing organizations.

The trouble with this realization was twofold. First, there was little readiness in business in the mid-1980s to entertain the notion that deep-seated psychological change was needed. Resistance and denial were the norm among executives and managers. The other problem was that no common-sense framework existed to explain this mysterious process to pragmatic business people; nor did I have enough background to explain it myself. Clearly, I and others were groping toward an evolved level of mental health. Western psychology, however, largely lacked this picture as well as a guiding road map.

New Theory from Synthesis

The combination of despair about consulting and interest in defining a road map set in motion the next several years of intense research and writing. Initially I found Alexander Lowen's work on defense layers of the psyche to be a key. His picture of growth at ever deepening levels produced a profound "aha." Suddenly all those journal entries made sense. Another clue was the stages of death and dying from Elisabeth Kubler-Ross. Her stages tracked the feeling states involved in inner growth, although there were important differences between physical death and the psychological death that leads to maturation. Another distinction between Kubler-Ross' stages and my experience was that the work did not proceed in a straight linear progression, from "denial" on through "anger," "bargaining," "fear" and "acceptance." Rather, there were stages within stages and a constant interplay of up-and-down emotions.

Much of the writing preparation involved hours and days spent poring over my journal notes, searching for patterns and characteristics. Eventually these became integrated with Ken Wilber's consciousness research, Arthur Deikman's merger of psychotherapy/mysticism and Stanislav Grof's consciousness levels based upon extensive research. Both Wilber and Grof are important figures in transpersonal psychology, the field that merges psychology with the spiritual traditions. My heavy debt to these five people, plus Evelyn Underhill's study of mysticism, is reflected in the appendix. There the various frameworks defined by each person are related to one another and to the stages in this book. Hopefully my synthesis represents a new naming that adds clarity about *how* one navigates the sometimes perilous inner route.

Other important sources for the synthesis included Carl Jung, whose work is the base for much of the transpersonal viewpoint, as is that of Italian, Roberto Assagioli. Insights about the tenacity and trickiness of our ego came from Fritz Kunkel, the German-American whose writings have been brought to light by John Sanford; A. H. Almaas contributed important concepts about "essence." My research also included mysticism, Native American Indian literature, feminism, some history and addictions treatment.

Two questions plagued me as I researched and wrote. One was how "the feminine principle" affected the inner growth process; ("Feminine principle" means feminine energies and qualities, whether residing in the female, the male or the universe) another question was how extensively the experience applied to the general population.

To understand the relationship between maturation and the feminine principle, Anne Belford Ulanov's work on adult growth and the feminine was particularly helpful. Linda Leonard, Marion Woodman, Shirley Luthman and Adrienne Rich were also key. Eventually I concluded that adult inner growth was synonymous with recovering our feminine energy as a species. "Feminine" here is defined in the traditional sense as associated with the unconscious, passive, intuitive and dark.

Today there is still much confusion about what truly constitutes feminine and masculine. A growing men's movement shows us that men too are in search of redefinition. As I read Sam Keen *(Fire In The Belly)* or Robert Bly *(Iron John)*, however, I see that both women and men are undertaking the hero's journey of "departure," from normal life, "descent" into the world of dreams, demons and darkness and "return" to creative contribution. To do so requires the deep personal growth of making the unconscious conscious, finding our "being" or passive side, accepting our vulnerability and putting our intuitive in charge. Such characteristics or processes have traditionally been associated with the feminine principle.

The importance of identifying this growth as essentially a recovery of the feminine in human nature is that the naming itself is a validation of some characteristics that have been denied or devalued by both women and men. To recover the feminine, however, does *not* mean to become soft and passive; Robert Bly suggests that some men became so mistakenly and thus must find their "wild man" side. The point is that the patriarchy has been lopsidedly balanced in favor of thought and action versus feminine feeling and being. Deep personal change requires recovery of the latter—a journey to the dark, inner realms where individual essence and a larger self reside. Healing a troubled world will mean wholesale recovery of this inner force, then balancing it with the outer. Feminine/masculine *balance* is the goal.

The fact that we are emerging from centuries of male dominated patriarchy explains why the inner journey is being demanded today of more and more people. Restoring balance by recovering the feminine and *integrating* it with the masculine is sorely needed within persons and institutions. Actually the journey itself is not new; studies of mysticism and religion hint at its ancient roots. What *is* new, however, are the studies from depth psychology that help explain it in modern terms. Also new is the growing realization that a shift in consciousness, based in profound personality reorganization, will be essential to coping with the present and future. Authors such as Alice Miller and John Bradshaw show how our current transition era requires looking at the dark side of parental beliefs that we previously accepted as "normal." It is literally time, in terms of the history of the world, for us to "wake up" to a different reality and way of being.

The patriarchy, it turns out, has perpetuated conditions of *learned dependence* that remain deeply rooted in our psyche. Only transformation at deep levels offers the opportunity to move us beyond such dependence. The journey also moves us beyond egocentricity, or a way of living that is defined by external opinions and standards. Moving through the inner domains requires considerable courage, perseverance and usually professional help. Those who refuse such growth are often the greedy, the corrupt and the arrogant. They are living examples of a stunted personality level, the egocentric person who has failed to mature psychologically. Yet the other side of the coin is that many people today also have a highly developed ego that allows them to plumb the unconscious without being overwhelmed. And ironically, it appears that those most wounded are leading the way to higher mental health. This is probably true because there comes a point where you either work things through or else you go crazy. The challenge before us on a societal scale is to move beyond the patriarchy to a level of functioning that has been unknown in the world today.

Merging Psychology and Organization Theory

The challenge to understand and describe how growth occurs occupied much of my time between 1986 and 1989. The manuscript went through several versions and revisions. Then, in 1990, through the impetus of starting a new business, I resumed reading management literature, especially the recent works on "leadership." There I saw, in the work of Warren Bennis, Burt Nanus, Harold Leavitt, John Greenleaf, Dale Waterman, Tom Peters and others, the focus on "the new leader" as someone with vision, flexibility and wisdom. Not surprisingly, I realized that these needed new leadership qualities were synonymous with the outcomes of individual transformation. The organizational authors, however, were missing a clear picture of *how* it could be developed. Peter Senge *(The Fifth Discipline)* suggests that "personal mastery" is one of the five keys to building a learning organization. Harold Leavitt ("Educating Our MBA's: On Teaching What We Haven't Taught") writes of business schools that don't begin to teach the things that come from a manager's internal world—namely, imagination, personal commitment and the deep belief that comes from the *soul.* Abraham Zaleznik, author of *The Managerial Mystique,* points out that a managerial ethic that stresses order and predictability, hobbles us from developing the visionary thinking and bold actions of leadership. None of these men, however, describes the path of psychological development that produces true leadership.

No one, it seems, has yet bridged the worlds of transpersonal psychology and current management theory to recognize the convergence of the two during the last decade. This book, about the turmoil of inner growth, begins to make that bridge, suggesting that there is an identifiable internal process. The process cannot be "taught" so much as mentored and encouraged. Having a clearer road map, however, should help many more achieve the higher ethics, enhanced creativity, vision and spiritual purpose so desperately needed in today's world. Understanding the process could significantly reform business school or leadership development curriculums and give added meaning to many individual journeys.

Beyond the merger of the transpersonal and leadership development, however, there are further exciting applications. Once we understand the underlying processes of individual growth, for example, we also have a new framework for understanding organizational change and learning. There is a direct correlation, in other words, between the deep learning that unfolds in the psyche and how that happens in organizations. This theme will be the subject of future work.

Beyond Turmoil: A Guide to Renewal Through Deep Personal Change represents a synthesis of existing ideas-research, the addition of my own experience and insights and their compilation into a self-help oriented book. Integrating these themes, naming the stages in a new way and expanding the existing knowledge amounts to a new model of human development. That model is compatible with and builds upon others. Because it is based upon so much more than just one person's experience, or even upon more than the results of original scientific research, I believe the book provides conclusive evidence that a new, transpersonal framework exists. Thus, this paradigm begins to reform, reorganize and restructure our approaches to a host of urgent problems, from business renewal to drug usage, alienation, violence, dysfunctional families and malfunctioning systems. What is especially hopeful about this new framework is the thought that massive healing might be possible. The new framework identifies human wholeness and what it takes to attain it in the present culture. We have barely begun to tap the potential of such knowledge. Such healing is needed to save our planet, to develop the undeveloped world without raping it and to create a quality of life where both personal fulfillment and maximum individual contributions can flourish.

One of the things holding us back from this healing process is the lack of acceptance within and without the behavioral sciences about this new framework. As Thomas Kuhn, author of *The Structure of Scientific Revolutions,* the landmark work on the evolution of scientific discoveries shows, the full development and application of a new paradigm does not take effect until it is recognized and considerable support exists for the new approach. Society is clearly at a point where it needs to develop this broad based agreement about a new way to view healing, change and growth. This book is a contribution in that direction. The applications are numerous; present problems far outstrip our capacity to treat them, yet each person who pursues deep personal change increases the possibility that the future can be vastly different.

Alice H. Mack, Ed.D
Tucson, Arizona, 1992

1

Despair
is a Signal:
How the Psyche Unfolds

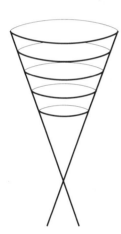

Margaret wasn't sure she could make it through the week. As a counselor for an Employee Assistance Program, she had barely been able to function lately. So far she had kept the sadness and shame at bay. But lately the crying jags came without warning. In the midst of a counseling session or staff meeting, suddenly she felt weepy and needed to be excused to compose herself. How could she keep going? What was happening?

Margaret was so tired of it all. For several years she had been seeing a therapist. The process seemed endless, however. At first she had been so angry with everyone and everything that she could hardly go to work. The way her boss spoke to her made her feel rebellious and unappreciated. Would he ever recognize her contributions? The therapy had begun to trace much of her anger to a family that still wouldn't talk about her father's drinking. Last Easter Margaret felt so fragile that she cancelled her family visit home to Virginia. She simply couldn't face them. Now she was feeling stronger, but the despair was like a ledge of sorrow that threatened to engulf her at any moment. Something must be seriously wrong with her, she concluded. How could she have worked so hard on herself these four, almost five years and still be feeling so rotten?

Margaret had been feeling anything but confident for several years. Seldom had she shared the depths of her experiences with others; friends didn't seem to understand, and work was not the place to discuss personal problems. Only her therapist knew the truth. Sometimes Margaret needed extra sessions, but even the weekly schedule was straining her budget to the limit. Her financial woes added to the despair. Yet she couldn't afford to stop the therapy either. Right now it was her lifeline.

When Margaret learned about the stages of inner growth, the weight of her burden lightened. The words for several of the stages, such as Anger/ Blame/Projection, Tension/Confusion/Conflict and Fear/Guilt/Grief, brought instant recognition and relief. Suddenly she saw this trying period as useful, even normal, rather than typical of someone deeply troubled.

Margaret's story is not unusual. Nor is it unusual that neither she, a trained counselor, nor her psychoanalyst, a competent professional, remained unaware of a process that affects so many. The sad fact is that Western psychology has been unable to present us with a coherent picture of higher levels of human growth. In the same vein, news reports describe the high incidence of depression in the baby boom generation. Such reports fail, however, to suggest that something deeper may be at work beneath the surface. Both depression and despair may be but a calling to inner growth.

A Mysterious, Complex Process

Carl Jung, the Swiss psychiatrist, was one of the first to name the process of adult growth in psychological terms. He called it "individuation." Jung knew that it was a major task of midlife to come to terms with our unconscious aspects or dark side, contact our spiritual self, and balance the feminine/ masculine. He concluded that a successful individuation process culminated in a person becoming aware of their unique purpose. Classically, the midlife passage occurs between ages 37 and 45, yet there are many variables in the process. Those younger may feel its pulls, and those older who have been busy with career or child rearing may delay the experience a full decade.

Even Jung, however, did not know how this process worked. In addition, he was not widely accepted or followed in his time, except by a small, loyal group. The mystical quality of much of his work, plus the spiritual tone that lay behind it, didn't sit well with the majority of the psychological community who were trying to prove that they were as objective and credible as the hard sciences.

When we realize that Jung died in 1961 and that his work has become popular only in the last 20 years, we have some perspective about the "youth" of psychology. Today major competition still exists among the behaviorists, the Freudians, the Jungians, the Gestalt school and others. The most recent challenge to the field has been transpersonal psychology, which builds upon the work of Jung and others. The transpersonal viewpoint merges ancient spiritual traditions and depth psychology. It provides us with a picture of adult growth that takes us beyond scientific rationalism. The transpersonal framework is a hopeful picture about the possibilities for human development, and it helps explain many growth struggles.

An Overview of Growth:
Despair and Losses

Almost everyone who undergoes deep personal change feels despair at one time or another. This is because psychological maturation involves "dying to ourselves" so that a new "self" can be born. Some, such as Roger, a doctor with a large practice, become immobilized for a time. At first he thought he could manage the deadening feelings, but he soon realized he was useless to his patients. Perhaps he would endanger them. He felt lost, lethargic and utterly hopeless about life. Concerns about aging dominated his thoughts; he feared he would never attain the research fame he sought. Several years ago he took a new appointment in a large Northwestern hospital. Things were going well overall, but the move itself felt like a loss of old colleagues and familiar stomping grounds. When Roger decided to get psychiatric help out of state, he did so only after fabricating a story about taking a leave of absence to pursue further training. He feared professional repercussions if people really knew the full story.

Tragically, people like Roger don't realize that they are not "abnormal." Some, like the Chief Executive Officer for a successful mail order business, commit suicide because they feel so alone. He apparently couldn't reconcile the demands of being competent and in control with his underlying depression. Yet becoming acutely conscious of "endings" is a distinct part of the stages of growth. Too many of us, however, keep all of this to ourselves. Both the doctor and Margaret, who had excellent professional skills, experienced unnecessary shame about a process they should be enormously proud to claim. The CEO couldn't bring himself to ask for help and chose death instead.

The agony of our ignorance is that people's suffering has been increased, even subverted because we haven't understood the rigorous demands of profound inner change. Many people turn away from plunging inward because they are understandably afraid; some are medicated or otherwise mistreated by doctors who know nothing about higher levels of mental health. In general, we have provided little cultural support for this most difficult life transition.

The linear view of how this growth proceeds shows clearly that endings are a large part of its unfolding. (Diagrams, pages 10 and 11.) The actual path, however, is cyclical rather than linear in our experience. During the first several years of *Initiation/Denial,* the introductory phase, we become mildly aware of changes. We may recognize that a wholesale evaluation is underway, but we are only being introduced at a surface level to deeper growth.

During the second trimester, the phase called *Separation/Disintegration,* endings become accentuated. Psychologically, we are being separated from the sense of self that we built from childhood. That sense of self, commonly called our ego, is mostly an outer shell that has been built up over the years. Through interactions with the world, people's responses have given

Four Phases

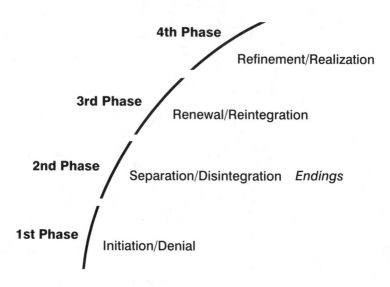

4th Phase

Refinement/Realization

3rd Phase

Renewal/Reintegration

2nd Phase

Separation/Disintegration   *Endings*

1st Phase

Initiation/Denial

us an idea about who we are and what we can do. Many messages have been absorbed unconsciously. Now that we've survived the initial years of adulthood, however, the time has come to expand our sense of self.

This new self will be larger than the "personality" developed earlier because it will eventually incorporate both the old and the new. Developing it will require a period of separating from many old moorings. Roles that we've played, places we've lived, skills that we've learned, relationships we've accepted, beliefs we've held—all of this can come into question or be ripped away. Excruciating psychic pain can accompany this experience; intense emotions are "normal." In a very real sense we are being stripped bare. It is the psychological "death" of an old self that is too small to accompany us further.

The years-long cycle of growth then enters a third phase of *Renewal/ Reintegration*. During this phase the new, enlarged self must be integrated with the old identity. We begin to feel alive again, ready for new things, although more endings can continue as we clear negative patterns. Apparently this enlarged self requires plenty of practice before it is firmly anchored in its new center. Finally, after many years of work, usually when we are feeling fine or "normal" again, there is a phase called *Refinement/Realization*. This is when mastery of our lessons occurs; here the changes we have made internally begin to show up as new projects or as the beginning of major life contributions.

Within the four overall phases of growth there are seven distinct stages of varying length and intensity.

Seven Stages

		Stages
	Vision/Purpose/Fulfillment	7
3 Years	Centering/Illumination/Expansion	6
7th Year		
	Being/Resolution/Acceptance	5
	Fear/Guilt/Grief	4
3 Years	Tension/Confusion/Conflict	3
4th Year (Crisis)		
	Anger/Blame/Projection	2
3 Years	Awakening/Questioning/Emptiness	1

The first stage, Awakening/Questioning/Emptiness, which contains both the seeds of deeper change to come and our responses, appears to last about three years. It is followed by another several years of incorporating the more difficult stages of Anger/Blame/Projection, Tension/Confusion/Conflict and Fear/Guilt/Grief. The fourth year of the cycle, according to Renaissance man, Dane Rudhyar, is a turning point. This is a probable critical state when growth either scatters and runs amok or else deepens and leads later to integration. The choices we make, in other words, to seek help, to buckle down and do the work involved in this inward calling, determine the outcome of the cycle. The experience of an outer crisis, however, is a common introduction to the work of this second phase.

Rudhyar also believed that the seventh year was both the culmination of what occurred earlier as well as the seed for a new seven year cycle (Rudhyar, 1975, p. 90). The diagram above and naming of the stages, however, indicates an eighth and ninth year of spiritual deepening, followed by personal mastery. Thus, there may be a total of 12 years from awakening to realization. Actually we need more research to determine the timing and duration of these stages. Obtaining valid data, however, is difficult since such data depends upon self-reports of internal experience. A compilation of such reports, however, would be extremely useful.

From Outer to Inner

Moving from initial symptoms of awakening, through deep loss and on to renewal, can be one of the most trying yet rewarding life experiences.

Levels of Self-Knowledge/Defenses

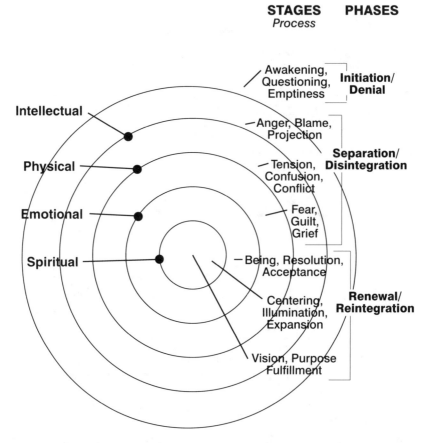

Because it has not been well understood and named, however, the process often appears to make no sense and have no end. Actually there is an orderly unfolding to the seeming inner chaos.

Much of the puzzlement arises from the fact that we are called upon to continually revisit the issues and people that wounded us in the past. Mother and father issues, for example, are seemingly dealt with in therapy only to recur months later. Once again we are required to clear ourselves of negative emotions.

The need for this repeated reexamination can be explained by the cyclical growth path which moves us through the defense layers of the psyche. Gradually we move through levels of self-knowledge until we reach the inner core of self. As we work our way through these layers, the barriers or boundaries are progressively shattered. This is commonly referred to as

Unlayering the Spiral

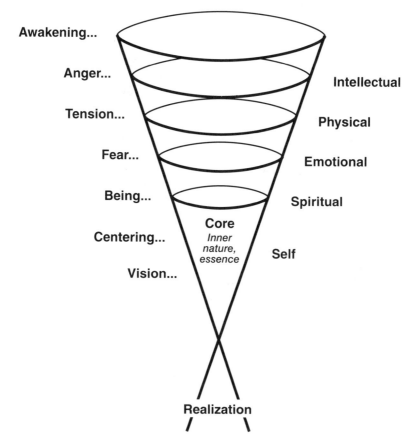

Awakening...

Anger...

Intellectual

Tension...

Physical

Fear...

Emotional

Being...

Spiritual

Centering...

Core
Inner nature, essence

Self

Vision...

Realization

"unpeeling the onion" or as unlayering ourselves. Once we begin to tap regularly into our self or core at the center, all of the levels can become integrated into a whole.

The circular nature of growth is portrayed in the diagram on page 12. It shows the four-part make-up of human beings—our intellectual, physical, emotional and spiritual aspects, plus the accompanying stages and phases. Much of the journey can be understood as the opening of our spiritual capacities. In order to do that, we must first loosen the constrictions of our egos, then dare to expose the defenses that have become lodged in both body and emotional levels. As we do that, we release and heal wounds from both family and the collective experience of history.

Another way to think of this unlayering is that of a spiral that starts at the top with wide circles, moving us downward or inward into ever deeper levels.

As we move into these interior regions, we must continually grieve; many of the losses are actually illusions about the way we *think* life was or should be. These thoughts, which have been built up and stored within our unconscious, including the cells of our bodies, are the result of social conditioning. Often that conditioning is at odds with our inner nature. Doing the inner work helps lead us to a life of inner peace, creativity, and the ability to love ourselves and one another.

As the spiral unfolds, we have the opportunity to recapture this inner nature, the essence of which we had as infants in a pure but undeveloped form. Now as adults, however, we must not only recover that essence, we must also strengthen it to become capable of integrating all four levels.

The fact that growth is cyclical and spiral means that it is hard to track our progress. Often we feel as though we are regressing rather than moving forward. Fortunately, as the spiral unfolds, the time spent digging out the dark spots becomes shorter and shorter. The greater depth we are working at, however, the more intense our emotions. The Fear/Guilt/Grief stage, for example, is much shorter than the several years of Awakening/Questioning/Emptiness, but the lower layer involves emotions that are the most deeply lodged and most potentially painful.

Further difficulty in tracking our progress arises from the fact that there are stages within stages within stages. As Margaret worked through Tension/Confusion/Conflict, for example, first she became aware, then angry, then confused and finally able to release memories and feelings about her father. At the same stage she experienced a similar sequence with mother issues, then some connected to an older sister. Throughout these months, the overall tone or sensation was one of Tension/Confusion/Conflict. She was attempting to integrate mind and body, yet her unfinished business with each family member evoked the entire sequence of stages as well.

Stages can also overlap so that characteristics that fit one stage seem to occur before or after. Therefore, the best way to use this "map" is as a general guideline. Knowing characteristics of each stage can be comforting, but interpreting them too strictly isn't helpful. Especially when people are in the middle phase of separation, descending towards the core, the work can seem unending. Gradually things do get better, of course, although there are many individual variations of how the experience unfolds.

Beyond Ego to a New Era

Another key to understanding the maturation process is to trace, in a psychological sense, how we evolve as individuals. The view of how the psyche matures helps us see that our present state of development, the patriarchal, is an incomplete state. The state of consciousness that we generally accept as the end state of adulthood is really only a partial development. In its totality, the path of consciousness can be seen as movement of the

Human Growth (Jungian)

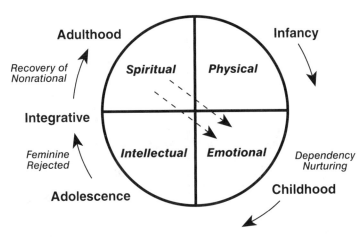

ego from infancy to childhood, then on to adolescence and finally adulthood as shown in the diagram on this page. That movement, as illuminated by the Jungians, takes us beyond our rational or intellectual powers, or an ego-based identity, to a higher development. Such a progression, however, has not been true for humanity as a whole until now. This is because the culture is still at a point where scientific rationalism and the dictates of the patriarchy affect our ability to complete the cycle.

The easiest way to trace this maturation process is to think of the human psyche evolving, clockwise, through its component parts—physical, emotional, intellectual and spiritual. Each quadrant can be related to a particular developmental period that, in turn, is related to the degree of consciousness attained. The diagram above depicts this cycle.

During infancy, for example, the child is not very separate from its mother or parents. In fact, the loveable quality we see in infants is a reflection of a state that is close to a pure but undeveloped essence. There is a lot of oneness with the parent.

As childhood unfolds, the child's separateness or consciousness grows, but there is still high dependence on parents for nurturing. Think of the young child who doesn't want mother out of sight, but later masters this fear. This is the *emotional* phase of our development; during it we do whatever is necessary to avoid pain or punishment in order to receive parental support.

Adolescence is the time when will power, self-discipline and rational control must be learned. We admonish children, for example, to be grown up, to become more independent and responsible. As dependency needs are curbed, the adolescent usually tests the limits of what it means to be in charge of themselves.

Civilization's Progress

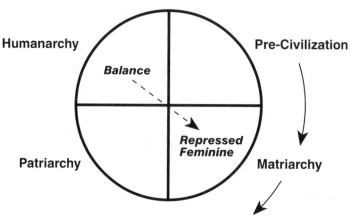

To accomplish this separation, however, the Jungians suggest that the former dependency ties must be rejected and suppressed. This means disowning the feminine or the emotional in order to "grow up." Such rejection is probably necessary so that the fragile ego won't be pulled back into unconsciousness.

Only as the spiritual quadrant opens during the *integrative* phase of development is the ego now strong enough to recover feelings shaped during childhood. In other words, during adulthood we are required to go back to the unconscious where buried emotions exist.   Before we developed a truly separate identify, we were not strong enough to take on this regression. We might have been overwhelmed, for the pull of the unconscious is strong enough to induce legitimate fear that going back will cause us to lose our way. Once we have a strong sense of who we are as persons, however, the ego can recover the "lost" aspects from the unconscious (Ulanov, 1971, pp. 66-70).

This overall pattern of individual psychic growth is a microcosm of civilization's progress over the centuries. Such a view helps us understand the limitations of the patriarchy. (See diagram above.)

Just as the physical stage of magical oneness characterizes the first months of life, so too were early humans barely conscious.   They were concerned mainly with physical survival.   This was followed by the development of specialized villages and the advent of farming that allowed people to stay in one place for longer periods.   This is likely the time when matriarchy reigned supreme. The dependency on the feminine that is characteristic of this period is reflected in the numerous Goddess symbols that prevailed.   Many feminist scholars are now recovering evidence of this lost time period.

As consciousness continued to unfold in the human race, however, the patriarchy took hold, synonymous with intellectual development in the adolescent.   In order to become more conscious, people had to suppress the emotional, instinctual sides of their natures. Without such suppression, they would have fallen back into the less conscious level of the matriarchal. Thus, society rejected the feminine, labeled it as inferior and something to be discarded. What lay below this definition, of course, was *fear* of the unconscious. We were thus taught to fear the "dark side" of human nature, the uncontrollable body and emotions. Such qualities were denied with a vengeance or displaced onto women. We were not strong enough as people and as a society yet to risk the next stage of going back into that emotional quadrant to recover the "lost" feeling side. Yet doing so is what makes us whole.

Present culture is now experiencing the limits of the patriarchy. We find ourselves at the critical three-quarters stage of growth that can move us onward toward the humanarchy. "Humanarchy" is my word for the period of time in the future when feminine/masculine balance and human wholeness will be the norm. Right now such a state of realization is the privilege of a distinct minority, yet as more people experience inner growth, they will pave the way for a potential quantum leap to the new outlook.

When we look at evolution in this basic way, it is easy to see how the patriarchy is such an incomplete stage of development. Western, rational consciousness, about which we have been so blindly proud for years, is nothing less than the adolescence of human civilization! To move onward toward the humanarchy we must recover the unconscious, the feared shadow side of self.

Making the Unconscious Conscious

As we can see from these explanations, the path to maturity requires becoming conscious of feelings and buried events There is much "digging out" required, particularly now when daily life is still laden with patriarchal belief. Unfortunately, psychology has given us the idea that only troubled people need to plumb these depths. Instead, the dynamics of deep personal change suggest that becoming conscious of both a personal and collective unconscious is essential for many.

Becoming conscious is facilitated by understanding what some 5,000-6,000 years of the patriarchy has entailed. The first thing to recognize, however, is that the patriarchy in and of itself has not been a bad thing. This stage in civilization has been essential to our progress. Especially when we remember the superstition that ruled the Middle Ages, it is evident that scientific rationalism, or gaining control of our intellectual powers, was necessary to achieve our current state.

The trouble with the patriarchy, however, is that the world view that emerged during it became the entrenched framework. Instead, it should be viewed only as a stage in our ongoing evolution. The failure to see the patriarchy as only a stage has resulted in many excesses that today threaten our very survival as a species. In other words, the ego state of development has too often failed to undergo the moderation of further inner growth. Greed and corruption, for example, are reflections of people who have not matured. The spiritual component in such people has failed to open while the acquisitive, selfish desires of the ego have gone haywire. Many of the evils of the 20th century can be attributed to persons who have failed to truly grow up. They become fixated upon materialism and the lust for power.

At the tail end of the patriarchal epoch came the scientific revolution some 350 years ago. With scientific rationalism came attitudes about our "right" to control and conquer nature rather than live harmoniously with it. The delicate balance between humans and nature has repeatedly been endangered the last 100 years because of these attitudes. Pollution, toxic waste, deforestation, overbuilding, lack of planning and other forms of plunder threaten our future. As the decade of the '90s unfolds, finally it is becoming apparent that the earth is in genuine danger. We, as its custodians, are responsible for saving it.

Our psychological damage also needs healing. In fact, without becoming whole persons through inner change, we will be incapable of saving the environment. This is because immature people will continue to make unwise, selfish and unethical decisions.

The patriarchal outlook is rooted in a male dominated ethic that values form, order and structure at the expense of feeling, meaning and value. The feminine in general has been denied, devalued. Allegiance to the patriarchal order was secured with blind *obedience* to external authority, whether that be parents, husbands, political leaders, teachers or religious figures. The results of these male dominated principles being played out over the centuries are so pervasive that they are almost "hidden" from view; we take life under the patriarchy for granted. We see no other way to be, no other way to design our institutions, including the family, until we become aware of ourselves.

The result is an enormously unbalanced society that has reached the apex of masculine excess. Such feminine/masculine imbalance is clearly evident in our parents. In previous generations a man and woman came together as two halves of a whole. The man was expected to earn the living; the woman raised the children. While a couple constituted a certain wholeness as a unit, the strength of their roles prevented them from developing their opposite, balancing sides. Too often that meant that women stayed mired in a childish, dependent role while men escaped into unfeeling intellect. Many women, of course, exerted their strength in family dominance or in covert control of the man or children; many men played out a passive side in emotional withdrawal or alcoholism. Some homes were ruled by excessive discipline; others were missing it entirely. In addition, the dark sides that were not allowed in either parent were picked up subconsciously by the children. Stereotypical roles and expectations inhibited both women and men from true mental health and balance.

Only recently have male/female relationships incorporated shared parenting, dual wage-earning and more egalitarian roles. Today's parents are working out new definitions without benefit of models. Most are doing so as they also try to deal with the dysfunction that has been perpetuated from generation to generation. The corresponding privilege, of course, is that today's middle-aged are also the first generation to finally make this material conscious. We are the first to have choice.

Besides the feminine/masculine imbalance that inhibits wholeness, the patriarchy has contained some disastrous, hidden beliefs about parenting. These are especially difficult to uncover and accept. So strong is the expectation that we *should* love our parents, so great is our need for their love, that we feel bad or guilty if we challenge that upbringing, even it if contained severe abuse. There are strong pressures to maintain family secrets. Swiss psychoanalyst, Alice Miller, has produced several seminal works about this prohibition. Her writing and John Bradshaw's (*Bradshaw On: The Family*) help show us the effects from being raised in families with "traditional" child rearing attitudes. Such traditions include the idea that parents are always right, that children don't have rights or deserve respect, that too much tenderness might be harmful, that a child who really feels good about themselves is "too big for their britches," and that the truth cannot be told. These expectations produce harm.

The largest parental commandment of all, as Miller points out, is that "Thou Shalt Not Be Aware" of what your parents are doing or have done to you. This commandment is what must be overturned in the process of deep personal change. Beyond the physical and sexual abuse that is coming to light, we need to recognize the psychological abuse that occurs from parents who held "traditional" child rearing ideas.

Thus, the difficult task of inner change demands that we become conscious of background forces. Those forces have been both parental and societal. Hidden in our unconscious, in other words, is the evidence of *violence* that was done to us, often unwittingly, by parents who themselves were raised under their own *unexamined* prescriptions. The word *violence* conveys a broad range of effects, from psychological damage to the physical effects of beatings or sexual abuse, that many of us would find in our backgrounds if we dared to look.

To be violated means to be denied your personhood in any way. Since society today has never functioned at the level of full personhood, it follows that almost all of us have suffered from the "violent" parenting of the patriarchy. Almost no one was raised as a child with regard to their innate essence. Becoming aware of these issues, of course, can naturally threaten parents to the hilt. The current transition period places enormous strain on relationships between parents and children.

Nonetheless, the task before us as individuals and as a culture is to become conscious of negative beliefs. Almost everyone has been the unknowing victim of learned helplessness that keeps us dependent upon external sources of love. Today, the strength of that dependency is played out in addictions to substances, relationships, possessions, work, status and various activities such as shopping.

Beyond our individual struggles, there are many indications that the culture as a whole is becoming more aware. Many historians, for example, plus feminist scholars and some religious leaders, are reinterpreting history. While they seem to threaten the existing order, they also show us how the feminine was derailed as the patriarchy took hold. Goddess figures and female spirituality are being recovered. Matthew Fox, a Jesuit priest, writes about a spirituality based in celebration and creativity rather than sin and punishment *(Original Blessing)*. Such reinterpretations sometimes make it sound like history took a wrong turn. Actually, when we understand how the psyche matures and that recovery of an earlier, unconscious phase is critical, it is clear that there was no wrong turn. Repression of the feminine, the unconscious and the darkness was to be expected. But so too is its recovery now overdue.

The Hope of the Baby Boom Generation

Much has been written about the baby boom generation and how their progression as a huge bulge in the population has affected everything, from buying habits to mores. Seldom mentioned, however, is the significance of what might happen when many of them undergo deep personal change.

Baby boomers represent the first generation that has had a chance to pursue higher human growth en masse. They do so amidst the background of a field of adult human development that is less than 35 years old. Thus, we have barely begun to know what optimum human behavior involves. People in previous generations, especially those before World War II, did not have the economic freedom or the cultural support to do this consciousness raising work. Those parents were, for the most part, too busy earning a living to pursue notions about human happiness and fulfillment.

The fact that full maturity has so far escaped us as a species is also the reason why some current experts, especially those in addictions treatment, claim that 90-96% of us come from dysfunctional families. (To be dysfunctional means to live with a set of rules, roles and behavior that produce "disease" and confusion rather than growth and health.) The statistics about alcoholism, abuse, drugs, violence, eating disorders, depression and other maladies bear this out. Widespread malaise is characteristic today. While some of this may be attributable to true breakdown, the statistics are also symptomatic of the urgent need to heal ourselves. It is no longer so possible to hide things, and it is time to get on to the next stage. Baby boomers and their immediate predecessors are the pioneers in this psycho/social revolution.

When people begin to dig up painful memories, some appreciation for how new we are at becoming more mature becomes especially important. Sometimes children need to "have it out" with parents, but mostly they need to grieve. And they need to remember that parents were parented by others. The irony during this painful transition is that we are judging past parenting by an impossible standard. That standard is a picture of human health that has yet to be accepted as the norm!

At some point in the future, it is likely that people in their early 20s will experience the spiritual unfolding that is now occurring to the middle-aged. Even now there is evidence that some young people undergo spiritual emergence before establishing careers and families. Only further research can bear this out, but it seems likely that our spiritual quadrant could open sooner if there was not so much repression and denial in the first place. Because so much has been suppressed, however, and because society as a whole has not advanced, we now usually don't do inner work until middle-age. Given our current level of cultural development, in fact, there are many who have missed or will miss this experience entirely.

The more people who delve inward, however, the easier it will be for others. As each of us becomes truly healthy, we affect those around us. Most importantly, we stop perpetuating the norms of the patriarchy. We begin to live and act differently. The great hope of the baby boomers is that their numbers and their opportunity for awareness will make a significant difference to society's prospects for true maturity and wisdom.

Befriending Our Pain

Part of the reason why deep personal change is only now becoming "popular" is that it involves facing our pain and suffering. Such a prescription runs counter to a society devoted so completely to pain avoidance. If there is one major attitude that helps us unfold, it is the early acceptance that pain can be a friend, not an enemy. Whether it be actual physical pain or the psychic pain of loneliness, despair and boredom, the existence of pain is evidence that our bodies and our souls are seeking purification and wholeness. Instead, however, we are taught to deny and stay in control, to be strong and not to "feel sorry for ourselves." But there is a huge difference between feeling sorry for yourself and the courage of admitting pain. In fact, not facing the pain may mean succumbing to physical illness, remaining addicted or becoming stagnant and embittered in older age.

When we "befriend our pain," we allow negative emotions to emerge, thereby freeing this blocked energy. The imprint of the memory that caused the pain is thus healed. This is particularly true during Anger/Blame/Projection, Tension/Confusion/Conflict and Fear/Guilt/Grief. Behind this purging, however, lies new self-knowledge, forgiveness and acceptance. The only way out is to go through it. Hence, darkness and fear can be transformed.

We must, then, find safe ways to vent the negative emotions that have been repressed for so long. We must get over the idea that to seek help is a weakness, or only for those with problems. When we understand the rigors of adult growth, just the opposite is true. Those seeking help are the courageous, although there is also a time to move away from such support. Reaching out, however, helps assure us of personal renewal. Admitting our need also contributes significantly to overturning patriarchal darkness. As Robert Johnson, psychologist and author of several books about inner work says, "Feelings are messy. They get in the way of building a civilization. Therefore the patriarchy tried to dismiss them." The time is ripe, however, to restore balance by recovering feelings and befriending our pain.

2

Is This
All There Is?

Subtle Beginnings Propel Us Inward

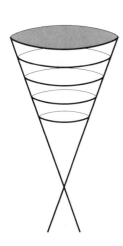 Michael was an airline pilot in his late 40s. Several extramarital affairs in earlier years had contributed to a bitter divorce. But now, three years later, a second marriage was relatively secure. His wife, Beverly, was a Realtor with poise, a quiet sense of humor and considerable financial independence. Lately, however, Michael was tempted to stray again. Recently he'd spent a weekend with Kay, a pharmaceutical sales representative he'd met in a bar in Kansas City. The brief fling left him feeling confused and guilty; he knew he loved his wife, but he was also intrigued with Kay. Fortunately, she had not pursued the relationship. Michael brooded about her for months.

There were other indications that Michael was not his usual, happy-go-lucky self. At one time the airlines had seemed the only job to have. Pay was excellent; time off was generous, and working conditions were good. Now, however, he found the cross-country junkets boring; after a flight he sometimes drank too much, especially if he was "deadheading" home rather than flying as crew. As remorseful as he felt afterwards, the binges helped him forget, briefly, that he was vaguely dissatisfied with almost everything.

Michael particularly dreaded coming home to an empty house when his wife was working. For some reason, he always felt lonely these days. Many empty hours were spent daydreaming about owning a sailboat. But buying it seemed out of the question. Beverly's career was firmly established in a town far from the coast; in addition, they had become victims of high living standards. Michael began to wonder about some of the trappings, such as the spacious, Tudor home, several expensive cars and a country club membership on top of hefty child support payments.

During his stretches of days off, Michael resolved his restlessness by following the stock market and working out at the gym. Finally he joined a men's group at the local church. As they explored feelings, roles, and stereotypical expectations of manhood, Michael realized he had never really developed intimacy with anyone. He felt gypped about not having had close men friends; furthermore, he was sadly puzzled about his relationships with women. He also began to question whether the security of the airlines was worth the price he was paying.

Michael was exhibiting all the first-stage symptoms of deep personal change. Among the clues are a variety of troubling feelings that eventually produce a thorough self-evaluation. Usually the first signals, however, are ignored. Questions are raised without taking action. We may be particularly puzzled about being dissatisfied because we've "arrived" financially or otherwise. Yet despite achievements, a tiny inner voice is beginning to ask, "Is this *all* there is to life?" To quell the discomfort, often minor changes in lifestyle, work or relationships are made.

In addition, mystical events, buried emotions and energy charges to the body may break through everyday consciousness. Their appearance tells us that a different level of reality is stirring below the surface. As we move in and out of looking at things more deeply, however, we retain our denial mechanisms. Our hope is that life will continue as before. At this stage we may glimpse some of our "unfinished business," the unresolved personal issues within us. But dealing thoroughly with them will only come later. This level is characterized by experimentation with change. We merely flirt with going deeper without a commitment to take the plunge.

The initial several years of midlife growth constitute a subtle *awakening*. Although we may not realize that anything special is happening, we are being introduced to both potential expansion and suffering involved in inner growth. This period of preparation is still based upon a self defined by external sources and cultural roles. The introduction amounts to a preparation for penetrating the barriers of the psyche.

IDENTIFYING CHARACTERISTICS

1. Changes begin; life continues as before, almost

Only in retrospect did I realize that the first several years were full of subtle signals. I barely noticed them as significant until I reviewed my journal much later. At the time I had no idea that I was beginning a long, demanding journey. After reading several books on "midlife crisis," I concluded that an evaluation of life would, of course, be healthy. During these initial years, however, such evaluation was mostly intellectual. I thought a lot about things, but I didn't feel much pain. In an outward sense, life continued much as it did before. Much of the reason it did, however, is that I wanted it to be that way.

At this level our psychic defenses are still pretty much in place; we're not ready to rock the boat very deeply. Michael, for example, had an affair, drank too much and questioned his career with the airlines. Each behavior was symptomatic of dissatisfaction with the status quo. Nonetheless, he was not yet ready to face the consequences of radical change.

2. Questioning values, lifestyle, choices

The restless questioning that typifies this stage incorporates almost every aspect of life. Amy, a bank officer, adapted her corporate planning skills to making a personal review. First she made endless lists about financial goals, career options, desirable qualities in a mate and important life values. Then she compared current lists with goals from her 20s. The comparison made her uneasy. She wasn't so sure anymore that the earlier goals were still valid. What did the discrepancies mean? Had she been wrong before, or was she merely wiser now? Was she compromising? Furthermore, did she really want to be married? What about a baby? Amy felt slightly cheated that the questions were occurring just as she had completed her "dues-paying" years. After all the hard work, why was she asking now, "what do I really want? What matters most and least?" Why was she second-guessing herself at this point?

Beneath Amy's quiet struggle was the overriding question that ushers in a deep change process that usually accompanies midlife growth. "Is this all there is to life?" That one question, if we dare ask it, actually heralds a profound search for deeper meaning. The second half of life will be barren without conducting the search, but when we first ask the question, the emptiness feels surprising. The things we thought would bring us happiness no longer suffice; the realization makes us feel cheated, caught off guard. During our 20s and early 30s we likely invested considerable time building a family, attaining skills or forging a career. Our focus was largely outward, but suddenly these external achievements feel hollow. Thus, we question goals, values, relationships and the choices that led us here.

Some people delay this questioning until their child rearing responsibilities are completed. One woman in her early 50s did not seriously examine what she wanted to do with the second half of life until she was smack dab in the midst of the "empty nest syndrome." She thought that her grief was all related to missing her two daughters and her mothering duties; she was disturbed that she was taking the loss so hard, but she didn't realize that feelings of loss accompany the midlife adjustment.

3. Initial changes made are minor, not major

Randy waited until his son graduated from high school before leaving an unhappy marriage and moving across the country. A new job and adjusting to being single felt like dramatic shifts. These major moves, however, were mere surface responses to deeper dissatisfactions. Often we hope that outer changes will make "the" crucial difference. Instead, such changes are usually only the beginning of change. There are many examples of major external changes that turn out to be minor emotional adjustments, including divorce, job changes or marriage. Even divorce can be a superficial response to the demands of personal growth, for many people leave partners without dealing with underlying emotional issues. Randy, for example, knew that his marriage had been sour for years. Leaving it was welcome relief from the burden of pretense; understanding real causes, however, would have to wait until he had more courage to look inward. For another man, getting married in his 40s after being a swinging bachelor seemed the answer to fulfillment. When the baby came soon afterwards, the futility of thinking that wife and child were the answer became apparent. Eventually his recovery from alcohol and drug abuse set him on his true path.

Another common response to gnawing dissatisfaction is to make a job change. Teresa was a marketing analyst who decided that a career move at age 42 would "cure" her restlessness. For a while the new position did assuage her yearning. She loved the romantic southern city and the challenge of being part of a startup operation. Several years later, however, she was still dealing with emotional issues of long standing. Making the job change had not been a wrong move at all; it just hadn't solved deeper questions.

4. Buried emotions break through

I was surprised when the anger and hurt bubbled up out of nowhere. Why should I be reacting now to a relationship that ended several years ago? Yet, for no apparent reason, I found myself sobbing quietly on the couch one evening. Memories engulfed me. The second time the emotions broke through, I was with a friend. Something he said triggered unexpected tears. Feelings of abandonment and betrayal emerged. As he attempted to soothe the outburst, my friend suggested that it might be time to find a therapist.

Soon I was enrolled in a weekly therapy group. There I learned that I *did* have feelings and that I had a "right" to try to get my needs met. Most importantly, the group taught me that many of us were struggling with similar issues. Despite huge differences in background or specific hurts, other people's pain and insights were helpful. I could identify with the divorcee, the struggling management trainee or the angry husband. I no longer felt so alone and different. After a year with the group, I felt well enough to leave it. The abusive past relationship felt healed. Later I would see that the coping skills I'd learned were only the tip of inner changes.

The fact that buried feelings start to emerge should not be surprising. By the time we reach adulthood, most of us have become experts at repression. One reason is that our culture has allowed little room for emotional expression or values. To be emotional in this society, to exhibit strong feelings, has been taboo.

The other reason for repressing emotions, however, is that repression appears to be a "normal" stage of human development. As we saw in Chapter

One, the search for adult identity requires a certain amount of emotional suppression in the service of gaining rational control. Such rationalism then carries us through the vocational and family tasks of early adulthood. What our society has lacked, however, is a clear view of *the next phase* of growth after we become rational adults. The emotional clearing work and spiritual emergence phase has been a missing component.

During the initial stage of inner growth, we begin to recover these "lost" emotions. Usually we are unprepared for the turbulence; it makes us feel out of control. Actually what is happening is a healthy emotional outbreak. Beneath the surface is a self that could not allow the repressed material to surface unless we were getting ready for something deeper.

5. Personal growth focus versus professional

Group therapy showed me there was more to life than career and achievement. Gradually I realized that the quality of the journey was as important as end results. For years I'd been a task-oriented workaholic, combining fulltime jobs with night school and weekend study. Later, there had been long days as I served out my self-imposed consulting apprenticeship. Now I reduced the work hours. Instead of usual work-related texts, I read more personal growth books. Such volumes as M. Scott Peck's *The Road Less Travelled*, helped subtly shift my values. "Finding inner peace" now became top priority.

Soon I noticed that other people were making similar changes. Several discussion groups I'd joined were more and more focused on the word "spiritual" as the defining nature of this quest. Most of us dared not use the word too freely. This was the early 1980s; talking about it in business would have made us suspect. But the inhibitions stemmed as much from the fact that we barely understood the search ourselves. We couldn't say "spiritual" easily because we remained tentative about what it really meant.

6. Subtle shift inward

An increasing need for inner reflection and time alone is closely related to the shift from a professional to a more personal focus. In this initial stage we may experience it as a periodic craving for retreat and withdrawal. One woman teacher felt so adamant about such time that she purposely scheduled a weekend alone every six weeks. A local camp provided the low-cost retreat accommodations. In addition, one day of each weekend was hers alone while her husband cared for their two young children. These were the bargains struck with a supportive husband before she agreed to have a family.

Finding alone time is considerably easier for single people, yet even dual-career families need to recognize the need for escape from overwhelming pressures. As inner growth unfolds, there can be a strong hunger to escape from the daily grind, to be responsible to no one but ourselves. Many of us yearn for the opportunity, now and then, to read, swim, write and drift through the days. Giving ourselves up to this kind of unscheduled time is partly the need to assess and reflect; partly also it involves experimenting with internal rhythms. Both consciously and unconsciously we are attempting to become more attuned to an inner voice.

7. Mystical experiences or unusual external signs occur

Entry to inner growth and maturation is often accompanied by a mystical experience. While many in the population claim such episodes, we seldom talk about them except in hushed tones to a trusted friend. These external signs can be visual, sensory, or auditory. A sensory sign could be an energy surge to the body. Several traditionally trained physicians have described how such energy charges created dramatic changes in their lives. Robert Moss *(The I That Is We)* and Brugh Joy *(Joy's Way)* both turned to unconventional healing activities after being awakened to new possibilities through the body.

An example of an auditory mystical experience would be hearing voices. One of the most famous examples is Joan of Arc, who heard voices that guided her to battle. Most common, however, are mystical events that are visual in nature. People experience a dreamlike vision that seems symbolic, unusual and out of the ordinary. Whatever the specific type of mystical event, they all reflect "breakthrough" phenomena from a different level of reality than we ordinarily know. Such experiences have the potential to awaken us, can sometimes be frightening and often suggest the future.

Susan felt both assaulted and energized by unusual energy charges. Her eyes were wide with awe as she described how that first electric current had surged through her body, seeming to change her vibration level. She felt more powerful and alive than ever before. It was as though she had been ushered into a new plane of existence. Her boyfriend had been with her; he verified the unexplainable 10 minutes of shaking, heat generation and vibrancy that had come over her. Later, Susan would experience another period of energy surges. That one lasted 24 hours and seemed triggered by making love. She slept only two hours that night; as the hours raced by, she roamed the apartment, read, wrote and restlessly waited for dawn. The following day she felt creative, impulsive and full of energy. She lived briefly at an accelerated level before things returned to normal.

The fact that these mystical experiences occur spontaneously is apparently common; often we don't understand their meaning until later. Unless we have recorded them in a journal, both the memory and the meaning may be lost. One of my episodes didn't make any sense initially. One Sunday afternoon in 1980 I was listening to the stereo through the headphones. Unexpectedly I slipped into a state where I saw energy waves, colored crystals, huge eyes of wisdom and historical figures passing before me. When I say I "saw" these, it was from the space behind my closed eyelids; the scenes floated before me for about an hour. Finally, the closing image was of a male and female face superimposed by a unisex one in the middle; the faces were luminous, god-like figures of exquisite peace and beauty.

Afterwards I felt awed, elated and confused. To whom could I talk about this? Would I sound ridiculous? The urge to share was strong, for I knew that life at some basic level would never be the same again. I also felt strangely hopeful and expectant, but I had no idea what the episode meant. Soon I found a book that assured me that others had had similar visions. Most of them, however, had taken psychedelic drugs. My vision had come without drugs or alcohol, although the music was a catalyst. Only much, much later did I come to believe that the closing vision stood for the balanced feminine/masculine energy so desperately needed in the world today. Perhaps that image was significant for me because my life's work is dedicated to that change.

Another potential mystical signal during awakening can be a prophetic dream. Such a dream, if captured, can later be revealed as another *introduction* to new possibilities. One of mine was about "changing jobs and teaching about the tunnel." The dream made no sense until several years later when I began writing about the "tunnel" of adult growth.

8. Erratic behavior, trial and error, denial

Michael, the airline pilot, is a prime example of the erratic behavior that characterizes this stage. At times he reverted to promiscuity and alcohol; other times he pursued new self-development. Michael, however, was unwilling at this point to face his boredom with flying and the emotional void with his wife. He didn't understand the forces that lay behind his experimentation, and he risked much he valued by having an affair and drinking too much. Such erratic behavior can be hard on others; we can easily hurt those we love when we are still unconscious and confused.

The fact that people have the ability to be so "split" within themselves, however, should not be surprising. As we begin the journey to full-blown maturity, we have yet to face our shadow or dark side, nor has our mind become integrated with heart and body. Thus, we function at times as though we are two different people. One lives out of the light side and the other inhabits the dark. Reconciliation of these opposites is, in fact, one of the prime tasks of midlife growth; during this initial stage we are particularly prone to erratic shifts. We toy with new values, behaviors, energies and potentials without committing ourselves. The result is an up and down, in and out, trial and error effect. First we go one way, then another. We plunge into making changes, then we retreat. Dissatisfactions prompt us to pull away from the tried and true. Yet we also cling to the status quo, trying to convince ourselves that minor changes will solve the problems.

The symptoms of this first stage are very similar to those experienced by dying people as reported by Kubler-Ross. Just as terminally ill patients hope initially for cures, the introduction to inner growth is characterized by the belief that nothing is really "wrong" beneath our troublesome questions. Numerous pulls inward may appear, but our hope is that continuing on as before will make things smooth again. At this juncture we may be willing to raise the questions that recur throughout the journey, but we do not fully face them either. We remain in denial.

9. "Unfinished business," or unresolved personal issues appear

As we zigzag forward to the unknown, part of what we seek is a deeper level of contact with both self and others. In order to develop that new relationship, however, we will need to face the "unfinished business" that almost all of us carry into adulthood. These are the personal and societal issues that remain unresolved in our psyche. Some come from our particular dysfunctional family; others come from society. The fact that all of us have issues to resolve is partly attributable to being raised in a Judeo-Christian era that emphasized "sin and punishment" rather than goodness and celebration. Consequently, most of us bear a heavy load of guilt. In addition, conditional love has been the norm rather than the exception. Thus, we were rewarded for "right" behavior and punished for "wrong," but seldom affirmed for being truly ourselves.

Many of us bear the scars of a shame-ridden upbringing. Even for those from comparatively "good" families, our psyches have been affected by confusing and incomplete role definitions of female and male. Such barriers meant that our parents seldom had the chance to become complete persons. Those of us caught in this dramatic transition period have a special obligation to sort things out. Coming to terms with ourselves means examining the forces that have formed us—and moving beyond them to self-chosen roles and behaviors, not those dictated by parents.

10. Presentation of both potentials and suffering

Another indication that we are in a "previewing period" during this first stage is the presence of doubts and fears. We may sense certain potentials about ourselves, yet we fear them too. Barbara shyly admitted that her journal from this period contained fears about power, success and sex. She was especially concerned that she had too much sexuality. As she progressed through deeper stages, she realized that fears of these strong energies were understandable. In the early stages she was not yet grounded or balanced, meaning she had not become integrated as a whole person. Gradually she felt the emergence of a deeper center as she came to know herself. Until that expanded inner self evolved, however, she rightly feared the lures of an egocentric, sensual world.

Initially, then, we are presented in a positive sense with new growth potentials through renewal episodes, energy charges, visions or inner urges.

On the other hand, glimpses of "unfinished business" and the presence of fear reminds us to go slowly. Experiencing our own greatness comes only when we build confidence that we won't be pulled off center. In psycho-spiritual terms, at this stage, both raging emotion or the selfish interests of the ego can still overcome us. We rightly fear their swamping effect, for our descent to inner wholeness is still fragile and halting. Only as we continue the journey, several stages beyond this initial one, do we uncover the higher self that anchors us in a new level of selfhood. In the meantime, fear is the cue that we are ready for further growth.

COPING STRATEGIES

1. Beware of employing stronger defense mechanisms

Drinking more, working harder, having an affair or running away in some form are all temptations during this stage. In fact, they are almost classic midlife crisis symptoms. Such avoidance mechanisms may help us temporarily handle stress, yet seldom do they solve anything of substance; often they make things worse. If you do find yourself indulging, ask yourself what the behavior might mean. Then consider other alternatives that might help you face yourself. Yes, it is characteristic to resist change, to look outward instead of inward for answers, to want to avoid the issues. But no, it is not helpful to cover up too long or too hard through drink or drugs, overwork or romantic diversions. Berating yourself for these excursions is not helpful either, but their presence can be a trigger to begin soul-searching. It may also be the time to seek help--NOW, before the problems worsen.

2. Accept distress as normal

In a society geared toward pain avoidance and the myth that we "should" be both happy and in control, there has been little permission to admit the discomfort of inner growth. No one tells us that becoming whole, mentally healthy and mature may require some vigorous, decidedly uncomfortable emotional work. The journey inward would be eased if we welcomed stress and distress as indicators that a new level of growth is emerging.

3. Write your autobiography

How many times have you heard someone say they wished they could write a book about their life? The urge is a legitimate one, for each of us has a story to tell. And in the telling we usually develop new self-knowledge. There is no better time to write an epic about yourself than now. Use your own free form style, telling about turning points, important people and significant achievements, or try a more formal method. Progoff's *At A Journal Workshop* is a written guide to a very structured process; often workshops on this or other journal methods are offered in larger cities.

The purpose of the exercise is to get better in touch with yourself, not to be published, seen or heard. Writing an autobiography helps us look at the endings of one phase of life; it also sharpens observation skills for further growth.

4. Recognize that many events cannot be rationally explained

Someday we may better understand what human growth really involves, including multiple planes of reality and how "unreal" or mysterious events occur. At the moment, however, such things cannot be explained in rational terms; neither can they be proven with normal scientific methods, nor usually repeated. Such data or experience, however, can be verified through many first person reports. Inner experience can't be "proven" through outside observation, but it can be validated by others. Much of the benefit of inner growth, however, is to accept that life contains deeper mysteries beyond our comprehension. Accordingly, such events should be treated with reverence; they are gifts and should not be sought as ends in themselves.

5. Look for others with whom to share your experience

One of the most important things you can do for yourself throughout the years of this process is to share your experience. Unfortunately, we still suffer from fears of being called "weak" or "helpless." Thus, when we encounter personal battles or seek therapy, we often hide it. "Put on a happy face" seems to be the modus operandi. Yet admitting our need for others is a strength, not a weakness. Not keeping things bottled up inside is vital; gaining insight from others is helpful, both to you and the other person. Therapy groups, 12 Step programs, (i.e., Alcoholics, Overeaters, Nicotine Anonymous) discussion or support groups, women's or men's circles and simple friendships are all possible outlets. What each requires, however, is the willingness to reach out to others. As we do so, we need to admit our need for new answers and support. Sometimes these can be the hardest words to utter.

3

Recovering
the Dark Side:
Volatile Emotions are Normal

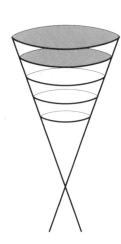

Throughout the week's vacation in Mexico, I slept 12 hours every night. During the day I stared at the ocean like a zombie; every few hours I swam. Was I exhausted from too much work, angry with the latest man or merely depressed once again? A partial answer came from several dreams. They portrayed scenes of loss and pain; one was a strong message to do some active grieving, but I didn't know how.

Stronger signals appeared months later. In the midst of a get-acquainted conversation with a new friend, suddenly my back was pinched in pain. I'd been telling him about myself. Then, half sobbing, half talking, I could feel throttled emotions being choked back. Why such an extreme reaction? I wasn't sure, but this time I knew I had to do something. Getting to the bottom of the symptoms was now urgent.

During the second stage of growth, we dance less around our issues and begin to feel more deeply; pain and suffering are more easily accepted. Torrents of anger may erupt easily, about events long past as well as recent slights. Or we may silently seethe below the surface, newly aware that others have mistreated us. Tapping into our anger appears a necessary first step to getting in touch with what has long been repressed. This "uncovering of our wounds" is like taking the lid off a host of emotions previously denied. As we remove the first layer, blaming others is a common first reaction. Only later, as self-examination and acceptance of our own part in the picture becomes clearer, do we withdraw our projections.

The theory behind this stage is that it involves establishing a sense of identity that incorporates our darker or "shadow side." This means enlarging the view of ourselves to include both negative and positive characteristics. Such qualities were repressed in the process of socialization. Raising these emotions to the surface can be unsettling; it gives us the feeling of being highly unstable. Cycling through a range of emotions, however, also leads to a stronger, more realistic sense of personal identity. We will need that strengthened outer shell in order to go much deeper.

IDENTIFYING CHARACTERISTICS
1. Willingness to face new truths

Marsha was finally waking up, at the age of 41, to some explanations about her history of choosing the wrong type of man. Initially the men came on strong, full of words and promises, but their follow-through was poor. In each case she clung to the relationship until it became verbally abusive. Had she been more aware, she would have realized that the men abandoned her emotionally very early.

Sean had been the latest whirlwind affair. Because he was a psychiatrist, Marsha thought, mistakenly, that he was a better candidate than usual. After several months, however, the familiar pattern recurred. Sean made a date for Christmas that he broke. Then he began reneging on other promises. Soon he was regularly breaking dates and asking for more and more "space."

This time Marsha reacted swiftly; she broke off the relationship abruptly. She also allowed herself to be angry about being betrayed. Always before she had bottled up the emotions, putting on a brave front to the world. This time she stormed. As she reflected later about what had happened, she congratulated herself on being able to recognize the discrepancy between the man's words and his actions. Previously she had accepted empty words that never quite matched actual behavior. Now she started asking serious questions about why she was attracting men of this sort. The anger soon gave way to grieving. After several crying sessions over a weekend, Marsha began to realize that her own capacity for intimacy might be seriously impaired.

Marsha was exhibiting one of the characteristics of the second stage of maturation, a willingness to face painful new truths. As we turn inward and look deeper, the masks we wear to the outer world start to come off. We no longer need to hide from ourselves. Marsha was moving beyond blame and anger to serious soul-searching.

2. Depression

Throughout all the stages of growth, depression can occur almost anytime. This is because depression often masks feelings that we fear bringing out. Depression, however, is particularly common during this second stage. One of the first signs that we are ready to push deeper may be such symptoms as sleeping longer, feeling listless or hopeless. Michael, the pilot, spent time brooding. Others report that a pervasive "blue funk" tells them they are enmeshed in uncomfortable, new territory.

During my Mexico vacation, I spent much of the week in sleep-filled depression. Luckily, I recorded a huge outpouring of dreams; these later helped me accept the "grief work" that needed doing. One dream, for example, featured a group of women surrounding me, exclaiming that they didn't know how to help me recover. Another dream was about saying goodbye to my parents. It suggested that I was being driven by parental beliefs and that I would have to give them up to be free. Still another dream scene was about "guns and arms" being used in a country like Thailand where they weren't needed. That message depicted my inner conflicts, yet it would be many months before I could shed the emotional armor. All of these dreams were related to the depression.

The fact that depression is one of the most common ailments in America today may mean that many people are ready for inner work. Depression is far more common in young adults than in their parents generation, and it is far more common in women. But such statistics may mean positive rather than negative things. If we understand, for example, that depression is characteristic of urges toward deeper growth, its presence may mean that many people are trying to get on with this work.

If we understood depression as the essential preparation for doing important inner work, we could use it as a vital signal. Unfortunately, too many people are merely treated with drugs without any attention paid to the inner psyche. Sometimes a drug helps people feel well enough physically to be able to respond to psychological treatment, but they also need help with digging deeper.

3. Strong shift to inner focus

Neither the Mexico vacation nor this first awareness, through dreams, of my unconscious life, made the depression disappear. Both, however, contributed to a sense that I had embarked upon an inner journey. Coming home to my 40th birthday at the tail end of the trip felt like a watershed. Whenever friends asked how Mexico had been, I replied that it had been quiet but important because it marked the time when I began to function "from the inside out." That statement meant that I had experienced the first shift to operating from a feeling level versus the mental programming that comes from parents and society.

To become even more aware of my inner life, a revelation that suddenly seemed so rich, I now became a serious journal writer. Before this, my entries had been sporadic; now I faithfully recorded dreams, insights, questions, random thoughts and feelings on a daily basis. That practice continued for another four years. It was as though I needed very much to talk to myself during this intense growth; more importantly, perhaps, is that I needed to *listen* to myself. I found I could do that best by writing; the journal became both companion and touchstone for the journey taking shape.

4. Outer crisis forces us back upon ourselves

The crisis that sent Bill, a welfare administrator, into serious self-examination, was the surprising stroke he suffered at age 50. For several months he was immobilized. Intensive physical therapy helped him recover the use of his right arm and leg. More important, the time off gave him the opportunity to assess how he was living. Coming face to face with his own mortality caused him to consider what really mattered.

Betty's trigger for turning inward was emotionally painful in a different way. Her boyfriend had landed in the detox unit at the local hospital for the third time when she finally began to question her involvement with an alcoholic. This time she refused to let him come home after his release; she also called a friend and asked about attending the meetings for Adult Children of Alcoholics she'd been hearing the friend describe. Finally, she began to look at her role as an "enabler" in the alcoholic cycle. Her own family's alcoholism suddenly came into focus.

Still another woman found herself with a suicidal teenager who forced her to start asking questions about the way she was living. The mother's high pressure career, too many late nights and too many men were partly behind the teen's rebellion. A successful stockbroker woke up when his wife walked out after 15 years of marriage. She took the children with her, and they remained uninterested in seeing their Dad, who had been an absentee father for several years.

Whatever the impetus, whether illness or emotional trauma, there is usually some outer event that forces us back upon ourselves. Suddenly the old ways we had of dealing with life no longer work. Something snaps within us, or breaks down, or sets off an alarm that gets our attention long enough to motivate the search for new answers.

Often this is the time when people first accept the need for professional help. My episode of unexpected crying, for example, the deep back pain and the choked-back screams, was enough to send me to the acupressure therapist. The combination of these physical symptoms and the earlier dreams finally told me that I had serious "pain homework" to do. It is appropriately called "pain homework" or "grief work" because it means facing things that have left their mark in the past. The events, however, were not properly grieved when they occurred; consequently we are not cleared of their negative effects. As time went on, I would discover the endless nature of this "pain homework." Some had childhood origins and some of it was universal in the sense that it was attributable to patriarchal wounds. At this point, however, I knew only that my system had become overloaded.

5. Outpouring of anger

The women's investment club had an uncharacteristic angry tone one evening. They were a monthly group, formed to help examine finances, learn about options and encourage risk-taking. Usually their discussions were business-like but personal. One evening, however, after a speaker outlined the dismal financial consequences for most divorced women, talk dissolved into angry tirades. Suddenly one of the women pointed out how vindictive they were being. Each woman was adding fuel to a fire of scorn directed at ex-husbands and men in general.

Once the anger was pointed out, they started to question themselves. Why were they so angry? And why were they all angry now, long after the early 1970s when they had first felt some rage in consciousness-raising groups? Most in the group believed in women's causes, but none was particularly militant. Most described themselves as "closet" feminists, meaning they supported women's issues without being very public about it; they all thought they genuinely liked men. Suddenly, however, their anger was boiling out.

As the discussion deepened, Kathy articulated best what others were feeling. "For years," she sighed, "I've been trying *not* to appear angry because I was hoping to make it in the corporate world. I didn't want to be seen as having a chip on my shoulder or as feeling sorry for myself. And I really thought I *wasn't* angry either, until I went into therapy recently. Now I discover I'm enraged about women being second-class citizens. I'm angry that feminine values and traits in *both* women and men have been denied, discounted and disowned."

This group's experience seems to support some therapist's claims that women need to purge their outrage about being victims. Yet there is danger in assigning this as a female issue. The men's movement is showing us that many men are angry too. Thus, the eruption may be characteristic of the second stage of growth. Anger is a signal that we're becoming more aware of both personal and social injustice. It is therefore important to have safe places to let the anger out, whether that be in therapy, a journal or in a growth group. The depths of such anger are rooted in the times we have not been seen or accepted for ourselves.

Both women and men suffer from not having their unique essence recognized. Another source of anger is the realization that the feminine, tender side of both women and men has been severely damaged. Women in general have not been seen, heard or valued because the feminine has been missing from the patriarchy; their rage may well be deeper and stronger, but both sexes have been wounded and need to grieve. Arguing about who is the more damaged solves little.

Elaine was a computer programmer who described the weeks when she got in touch with an entire cast of characters who had wronged her in the past. Her boyfriend caught some of the rage as she dredged up memories of everyone who had ever disappointed her. The memories involved seemingly small incidents as well as people long forgotten. Anger, revulsion and hurt poured forth; person after person and situation after situation was recalled in verbal outbursts and furious journal entries. She felt like a dammed up fountain that had blown free.

Elaine's experience was a purging of all the times when someone had not seen her true nature. Everything from being treated as a sex object to being unfairly punished or not regarded seriously flashed before her. When those episodes occurred, she had not been conscious enough to register the slights. Now the long buried reactions were coming out.

6. Discovery of personal wounds; flashbacks

Marsha, the young woman described earlier who began to question her relationships with men, had just moved from the East coast when she undertook a lengthy psychoanalysis combined with massage treatments. She was amazed at what the therapy process revealed. Her surprises included explicit memories about her own sexuality as a child and how her father had reacted.

Part of the mystery was that he had seldom touched her. Instead, her father had "sexualized" her, meaning he had reacted to her even as a little girl only when she was her sensual self. Marsha was surprised during therapy to recover images of being sexual as a youngster; she had distinct flashbacks of being a tantalizing child of three or four. But she was even more surprised to "see" how her father had encouraged that. No actual physical contact had taken place, but the mental flashbacks revealed scenes of his advances. She now understood these actions as those of a man unable to relate to females except sexually.

After the "seduction" occurred, however, her father usually spanked her or yelled a lot. His abuse was triggered by anger with himself for having sexual feelings about a daughter. The many times this happened set up the pattern of a "come on" followed by being hit. That was what she had learned to expect from men; that was what she had learned to know as love. Now, some 40 years later, Marsha was still attracting men who came on to her with great promises, then ended up "hitting" her in some way. The repetitive nature of this pattern was finally plain; breaking it was difficult.

Phil's story involved physical and emotional abuse. He was a leasing agency owner who went through co-dependency treatment to cure his depression. While at the treatment center, he uncovered vivid flashbacks of his father's abuse. In scene after scene, he had been chastised, sent to his bedroom for small slights and sometimes punched and slapped. The actual target of his father's anger seemed to be his mother plus the fact that marriage had meant lost career opportunities; the emotions became unfairly projected onto Phil. As Phil contacted his stored memories, he felt battered, as though he was being tossed back and forth in an on-going shipwreck. Much of the abuse had been verbal; the fact that it had been unjust meant that he absorbed it deeply, like a sponge that couldn't spring back.

Another man realized, much to his surprise, that his mother had been guilty of emotional incest. Her disappointment with her husband, who remained a small town hardware dealer, meant that she attempted to get her emotional and excitement needs met through the oldest son. Therapy sessions and considerable reflection revealed the scenario: She had played up to the boy as a coquette might; she leaned on him for decisions, praised him exorbitantly in public and compared him to her husband in front of others. Sometimes she also babied him. His memories were a haze of subtle improprieties that felt uncomfortable and wrong.

Anyone who has sought the type of professional help that raises memories is usually surprised, horrified and fascinated with the revelations. Did this really happen in my family? The fact that such pictures can be recaptured gives credence to the maxim that "there are no secrets." Even unconscious emotions can be picked up by children; each of us probably absorbed many from both parents.

During this second stage of growth, we are able to uncover material that comes from our personal unconscious. If there are emotionally charged events in our background, they start to surface here. Unlike some of the later stages, where nontraditional methods may be required, traditional therapy is generally equipped to deal with these childhood hurts.

7. Withdrawal of projections; self-responsibility occurs

The more that Marsha looked at her background, the more she understood what had formed her. The insights were complex. No wonder she ended up in unhappy situations. Her model (i.e., her father's suggestive behavior, plus his unsatisfactory relationship with a clinging wife) had been unhealthy. Marsha could now see how she had perpetuated that cycle; she confessed that she had probably even used sex to entice men. Consciously this was hard to admit. It was not how she wanted to see herself, yet unconsciously she had learned that using sex brought attention.

Further insights convinced Marsha that many of her present problems were related to intimacy fears. To love someone meant, in her experience, that you got hit. Often she picked men who would play that pattern out. Sometimes, however, she herself was callous and indifferent, treating men as sex objects too. That was the safe way to avoid emotional involvement and hurt. By the same token, she became newly aware of how tricked she felt when men wanted sex, then degraded it or women in general. That too was a common pattern. The insights were confusing.

Through the flashbacks, however, Marsha saw her own actions in a new light. The awareness gradually gave her confidence that she could someday find a healthy relationship. She also stopped blaming men for all her problems. Now she could see in what ways *she* had contributed. Consequently, her fears of intimacy lessened.

8. Acute loneliness can be experienced

Michael, the pilot who complained of dread about coming home to an empty house, is a good example of the loneliness for a deeper self-relationship that grows stronger at this stage. We may notice the loneliness earlier, but the ache behind it now becomes pronounced. Michael imagined that if his wife had been less wrapped up in her career and had more time for him, perhaps his loneliness would vanish. Actually, her actions would have made little difference; he needed contact with a level of self that is forged only through deep personal change. Only as he found self-companionship would he be able to relate better with his wife.

The emptiness that emerges at this stage is best described by comparing it with how you feel *after* you have made contact with an inner core. Afterwards there is seldom the same yearning for connection; the underlying longing for union becomes satisfied as you establish a sense of relationship with others, your inner self and the universe. While you may miss certain people at times, you are seldom, if ever, truly lonely. Instead, you are self-contained, content to be either alone or with others. To feel lonely at this second stage, however, is perfectly "normal." We are engaged in a wholesale search for missing parts of ourselves, especially our center.

9. A cycle of emotions; volatility characterizes inner life

George was both fascinated and frightened with his girlfriend's emotional ups-and-downs. Normally Stella's demeanor was one of calm reserve and good-natured reason, but lately this had changed. The fluctuations amazed her as well, yet she was pleased to feel enough trust with George to hold nothing back. One afternoon Stella was particularly moody. In a furious, angry outburst, she accused George of conducting a relationship that was going nowhere. Just as quickly, however, in the space of an hour, Stella was crying hard and then laughing hilariously. George wasn't sure what to make of this unpredictable behavior, but he was also envious she could tap the feelings so easily.

Such volatility is indicative of one of the most important second stage characteristics—surfacing once buried emotions. This is where we take off the mask of our persona, or public self, to discover repressed material. Not surprisingly, it bursts forth in seemingly uncharacteristic fashion. Instead of the denial and rationalization of before, here we begin to bare ourselves. Such revelations can help us accept in new ways our "shadow sides" if we are not overwhelmed with the outbursts. Often the shadow side is understood as the so-called negative emotions, such as anger, resentment, anxiety, fear, boredom, apathy, despair, guilt or helplessness. Yet "shadow" can also be the positive qualities we've squelched. These include joy, lightness, sexuality, courage, strength, agility and laughter. When we begin to accept this range of positive and negative emotions as part of us, then we stop finding those "forbidden" qualities in others. We withdraw our projections. We also become less judgmental, for it is easier to see that the struggle between dark and light, good and evil, goes on within each human being. The experience, however, can be tough on others. One man almost lost his job because his behavior at work was suddenly so obstreperous. Counseling finally gave him an outlet to vent the storm.

My own volatility was encapsulated in one long weekend I spent at a mountain cabin. Hoping to use the solitude to reflect about recent growth, I instead spent five days enmeshed in roller coaster emotions. My reading, writing and hiking were accompanied by joy, peace, elation, excitement, hope, anger, boredom, fear, guilt and gradually, a growing sense of terror. I came home one day early, in fact, because the panic was setting in. During the twilight hours I felt newly awakened to intense joy about being a woman; my morning walks made me feel strangely alive in a physical sense for the first time. Writing in my journal, I felt proud of what I'd done with my life so far; I was eager for next chapters. But I also cried deeply several times about the message of unworthiness received as a child. I despaired about the weight of male/female conflict that seemed embedded in me, and I knew that I'd been unbearably lonely during the week.

Experiencing this range of emotions can be explained, not as being erratic or out of control, but rather, as an expansion of how we define ourselves. During young adulthood we had a public image, an identity and a face we present to the world. Beneath this persona or mask, however, both positive and negative aspects of self were disowned. Such an outer personality, remember, is essential to developing rational control. During this stage we start to reclaim these qualities. As we allow these aspects to emerge, just noticing them without judgments, the effect can be one of cycling rapidly through a series of fast-changing feelings.

As perplexing as it may be to seem so unstable, allowing the emotions to surface is important. Doing so creates an enriched, multifaceted picture of ourselves. My mountain vacation had been confusing because I was unable to develop any great insights about inner growth. What I had done, however, was to identify a series of diverse moods, qualities, strengths and weaknesses. I thus expanded the picture of who and what I was. Such a revised self-definition is exactly what this stage involves; at the time I didn't realize that this revised image signified growth. Below the masks of our outward demeanor, in other words, lie our shadow qualities in both negative and positive form. When we can admit these, we end up cementing a healthy, more complete ego.

COPING STRATEGIES
1. Accept your unconscious as a "friend"

After my Mexican vacation, when a barrage of dreams broke through the depression, I knew that something important was happening. Some inner part of me was speaking with great intelligence; now I was more willing to hear its wisdom. Before I could accept the unconscious, however, I'd always been slightly afraid that therapy or a therapist would uncover something "awful" about me. Now I realized that only good could come from looking at the dark. Likewise, I was awed about the flashback scenes that revealed so much. At this point, in fact, the inner journey appeared as a whole new realm of discovery. Sometimes I laughed to myself that the opening to this inner landscape certainly beat watching TV soaps or reading tabloids. The drama I was uncovering was fascinating.

2. Be prepared to uncover family "secrets"

One of the biggest struggles about growth is to be able to see the truth about our families without blaming them forever. The line is a thin one. In order to be whole, we need to release anger about the verbal, physical or sexual abuse that may have occurred. Or the anger may be centered around the lack of emotional support received. Once the anger is therapeutically discharged, however, we need to stop dwelling on it. As Alice Miller points out, the proper attitude is *mourning* rather than blame.

The first step, nonetheless, is to be willing to look at what really happened. Those were the forces that formed us. For years we have carried their effects in our unconscious. Now we must begin to relive the episodes that left a significant emotional charge. Often reexperiencing those scenes can be a shock, particularly if there was severe abuse or incest; daring to bring this to light destroys our myths about the quality of that family life.

The fact that many more people than we imagine come from unhealthy backgrounds is sometimes hard to fathom. Experts suggest that some 90-96% of us were raised in dysfunctional families. This is not an unrealistic figure when we consider that most of us did *not* get our emotional needs met as infants and children; most of us were raised by people who were not whole people in the sense that we are now beginning to understand true mental health.

As we uncover these surprising secrets, it is helpful to know that we are not alone. Society in general is involved in an important transition; during it, many people are becoming conscious of what has been buried below the surface of human consciousness for centuries. Only people now in their 30s, 40s and 50s have been able, on a mass basis, to experience this kind of growth. Shedding light on those dynamics, however, does not always reveal pretty pictures.

3. Take time to get in touch with yourself

Amidst the demands of work, raising children and citizenship, time alone can be hard to find. Yet there is nothing more important than taking time for yourself. That can be anything from 30 minutes a day to longer retreats. Only in silence and solitude can we distill our experiences into wisdom; only by quieting the noise of the outer world can we hear the faint voices that help us move in new directions. One man, for example, developed the habit of driving for hours when he needed time out; another woman explored most of the West coast during a six-week vacation one fall. She came back knowing what she needed to do next.

4. Keep a journal

Taking time for yourself may include writing in a journal. If you have any inclination at all toward writing, then use this method to find out what you feel and think. Do not worry about the form, either inside or outside, although it helps to have a special notebook. *Do* worry about keeping it private. Having an uncensored place to record emotions, insights, dreams or secrets is important.

5. Look at male/female relationships as marvelous "teachers"

Stella's relationship with George, although unsatisfactory, acted as a strong catalyst to push her deeper into issues she needed to face. The reverse was also true. George finally went into therapy himself and they were able to share many insights. She was nothing like his mother and he was little like her father, yet there were certain dynamics between them that brought old family patterns to the surface.

Whatever difficulties women and men are having in relationships today, the truth is also that we help each other grow. We push each other's buttons; we bring out both the health and the disease in each other in order to become more fully human.

6. Accept fear or terror as "normal," even as progress

What appears to happen as we descend the layers of the psyche is that first we see a sort of mental preview of issues that require resolution; then we experience the fear of facing the emotions surrounding these issues. When the fear arises, it is important to acknowledge it as normal and natural. We may also need help to confront it, whether from therapist, friend or a workshop. By all means try not to keep avoiding the fear; the more you resist an emotion, the longer it persists. Fear can be among the most unwelcome of emotions, yet when we consider also that it helps us be prepared, we can accept it and use it to our benefit.

7. Don't miss the growth opportunity!

Musician, philosopher and astrologer, Dane Rudhyar *(Occult Preparations for a New Age)*, mentions the critical fourth year of the inward cycle as the time when a person either confirms the new direction of growth or else turns away from the whole process. At exactly what point we make this critical shift is unknown. The outer crisis we suffer in this stage, however, may well signify the crucial turning point. My realization that I needed more therapeutic help, for example, after Mexico and turning 40, probably occurred at this juncture.

In too many cases, the trauma that we encounter becomes a lost opportunity. One research chemist, for example, found himself unemployed at age 49. The layoff had been a political decision, not economic, and his ego was wounded. Neither he nor his wife handled the situation well during the 18 months that he looked for a new position. The role reversal incurred while she worked and he looked after the children was uncomfortable for both of them. After finding a new job, he still felt demeaned and confused, wondering about his lost dreams of youth.

This man's definitions of "success" needed to be examined, not to mention his emotions and his concept of himself as a man, but he had few resources available. The people around him were not helpful either; constant questions about his career and his direction were asked during the layoff, and no one ever suggested that an enforced time out could be a blessing.

While there is probably no one turning point that makes "the" difference, there are many ways to turn inward. Getting help, befriending the unconscious, writing in a journal and talking it out are all positive answers to the transformative seeds sown earlier. These actions set the stage for much heavier work as the critical third stage unfolds.

4

Back to the Womb:

Nontraditional Avenues to Growth

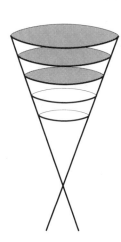

Occasionally screams pierced the air, or strange moans and wails in the small conference room; there was even a growl as the music rose to ear-splitting level. People lay at various angles to one another on their sleeping bags, foam mattresses or yoga mats while an attentive partner hovered nearby. This partner or "sitter's" job was to provide undivided attention and support to the "breather" during their two-hour session. Sometimes the partner offered more active help, such as holding someone while they sobbed, moving pillows into place to protect flailing limbs or helping facilitators push on a body part.

Initially the music was full of drumming, chanting and wild excursions. Later it turned dreamy and soaring; the group breathed quietly now, without sounds or much active movement. During the afternoon session, the breathers and sitters changed places; the whole group then later gathered to share their personal drawings and experiences. Each person's was totally different.

One man struggled to explain that he thought he'd experienced the shame that his parents felt while they were conceiving him. Rationally that made no sense, but he knew that strong guilt had accompanied their lovemaking. A woman groped with the words and feelings to describe a world of color, movement and loneliness. Her drawing was a mystery to her, but it looked very embryonic. During the session she had relived the birth experience, including her mother's alcoholism and being induced for labor. Both factors helped account for the current haze she felt. Other people reported sensations or visions of God, a sense of unity or knowingness, or past-life episodes. One had become nauseous during the session; several merely had a pleasant meditative trip.

This scene did not unfold in a psychiatric hospital, nor in some strange cult encounter, but rather in a workshop conducted by reputable, trained facilitators. The facilitators, usually from counseling or other mental health backgrounds, had been trained by Stanislav and Christina Grof who have developed a method called "holotropic therapy." The therapy, typically undertaken in weekend workshops, combines breathing, music, movement and an understanding of transpersonal states. The Grof method, which is also employed extensively in somewhat different ways by Jacquelyn Small and Greg Zelonka, often takes people into growth and healing experiences that are beyond traditional therapy. Stan Grof's work is the outgrowth of extensive psychedelic research that has since been substantiated by studying nondrug states. His investigations provide some of the most convincing evidence yet that deep personal change requires dealing with birth and death.

Such a birth/death struggle occurs at the Tension/Confusion/Conflict stage. Here we can experience flashbacks to childhood, infancy, birth and conception. The emotional work that must be done constitutes passage through a "tunnel" that both mimics the birth process and may take us back to reexperience our actual birth. Beyond the struggle, or below it, lies a new level of self or essence beyond the ego. Descending the spiral to this depth demands a new degree of emotional courage; most likely it also involves professional help, such as that received at a breathwork workshop or from another form of nontraditional therapy. Rebirthing, acupressure or other forms of bodywork are the most likely to produce results. (Rebirthing also uses breathing and other physical techniques to help the person reexperience the birth episode.) At this stage we are dealing with experiences that traditional methods neither recognize nor know how to treat.

Although one can experience extraordinary visions or surreal images while working at this level, the everyday feelings that accompany this stage are more that life is mundane, gray and hopeless. People are aware of inner struggle, lack of movement and being stuck. These "confusion" times represent past episodes when the body absorbed tension from assaultive and abusive behavior. The abuse may have been physical, sexual, emotional or several of these. As children, we armored ourselves against such onslaughts in order to survive them. Now, however, we are strong enough to raise them to awareness in order to find release.

This stage can be one of the most uncomfortable periods of growth, principally because it includes long stretches of feeling aimless, lost, even desperate. The lack of direction can be explained by the fact that our old, external ways of defining ourselves are loosening; but the new self has not yet become thoroughly grounded or anchored. We are literally "at sea" for a while, not knowing who we are, what we want or what life means. Fortunately, with patience and hard work, the emptiness gives way to a sense of renewal and body/mind integration.

IDENTIFYING CHARACTERISTICS

1. Expanded awareness of physical body; soreness, aches and pains

Becoming aware of my physical body actually began in the previous stage, on the mountain vacation. Groups of muscles and joints came alive for the first time as I hiked through evergreens and aspens. Now, as the growth process deepened, I often felt soreness that was not related to aging or illness. Usually the signs appeared just before, during and after a therapy session. It was as though my body "knew" that another session was imminent; sometimes I arrived for the appointment and merely pointed to the area that ached.

The physical ailments were positive signs that I was ready for more healing. Symptoms ranged from back pain and momentary paralysis, to terror and fear lodged in my pelvis and stomach. Behind the physical distress was both physical and psychic pain ready to be released. Ken Wilber, a prolific author about states of higher consciousness, suggests meditation as a way to become aware of these bodily tensions. I doubt, however that I could have done this work without a physical approach and sound therapeutic assistance.

2. Feelings of paralysis, lack of movement, being stuck

I cried my way through piles of Kleenex the winter that this stage unfolded, incredulous that this much suffering could be buried inside. By now I was desperate to relieve it. Release came often on the acupressure table, yet the days wore on into an endless gray period. I felt as though I was wading through internal molasses. "Being in the muck" again is how one friend described it; laughing at our mutual despair helped us endure it.

The explanation for the feelings associated with this level goes back to childhood. As children, we froze in terror when assaults to our physical or emotional being were inflicted by parents. Those "big people" were themselves unaware of their own internal conflicts, so much of their anger or hostility was projected onto us.

The degree to which we protected that childhood self by freezing our reactions depends mostly upon the health or dysfunction in one's family. But probably everyone deadened themselves to some extent. During the process of maturation, however, we become newly aware of those wounds to our body or psyche; freeing ourselves from their freezing grip is indeed a struggle.

3. Feeling aimless, lost, without direction, disinterested

In both personal and professional ways, I didn't know who I was or what I wanted during these months. Interest in work or play was nonexistent; I did the minimum to get by and still earn a living. Unsure and befuddled, I was unable to make decisions. Always before I'd been a goal setter and a high achiever. Now I couldn't plan anything, nor was I sure that much about life mattered. The days passed as though I was mired in a bleak vacuum, full of nothingness and drabness. This horrible gray period was worse than any previous depression; it was mental and emotional constipation. Sometimes I came home from work early and just cried the rest of the afternoon.

4. Changes in bodily functions; becoming embodied

Not everything was bleak. Small outward gains actually signalled physical changes occurring underneath. As I cleared the bodily blockages during therapy, a raging case of premenstrual syndrome (PMS) improved. My metabolism also changed; I could eat more without gaining weight because my system was more efficient. Despite feeling such despair on the inside, people reported that I appeared softer, prettier, more peaceful. The reason was that I was becoming more embodied. By resurfacing the original pain, I was reclaiming whole areas of a physical self that had been shut down, numbed or deadened.

5. Flashbacks to family "double binds" or emotional repression

Emily used a combination of acupressure and rebirthing sessions to work on herself. Rebirthing is the reliving of one's birth in a physical, emotional and spiritual sense. Generally, a therapist or rebirther helps a person get back to this primal experience through deep breathing, guided imagery and the encouragement to let go of negative energy or pain that might have surrounded an event.

It is difficult to describe rebirthing adequately in words, but Emily shared vivid details of how scene after scene from her family's past emerged in therapy sessions. First, the therapist used gentle touch on certain points to move the blocked energy. The movement activated a mental image, and moments after the scene appeared, the long denied pain came up. Emily gasped for the courage to allow it to surge through her body.

The therapist's presence made it safe to reach for the terrifying sensations. Each one of these flashbacks represented a wound in her psyche; each reliving and release meant a healing. The beauty of this physical approach is that neither Emily nor her therapist needed to "know" in an intellectual sense what family memories were important. Working with energy flows means that the body itself reveals the incidents or wounds that need to be healed.

During those mental flashbacks, Emily "saw" how she had been caught in the cross-fire of her parents unexpressed anger. Reliving them made her aware of how she had been in the middle, feeling terribly afraid because neither parent offered safety. Other scenes replayed episodes where someone said one thing but really meant something else. Words of love, for example, were accompanied by looks of hatred. Now Emily could see the sharp contrast between the conscious and the unconscious message.

Awareness of the double messages explains the *confusion* we feel at this stage in an outer sense. There actually were two conflicting messages, the spoken and the unspoken. As children, we're not sure which to believe, but the body registers the truth of the unspoken. This creates a double bind.

Parents may tell us, for example, that we are loved, but they are seldom honest about the anger, confusion or hostility they felt about some of our behaviors. Furthermore, they did not know how to tell us they hated certain of our behaviors but that they did not hate us. Thus, we pick up these supposedly "hidden" communications and store them as confusion.

Since our culture has been masterful at repressing emotions of all kinds, hardly anyone has been untouched by these double binds. They are built into the very fabric of our child rearing practices and institutions. In dysfunctional families, however, the dynamics are stronger and more damaging. Alcoholism, for example, is a situation loaded with confused roles, game playing and misplaced blame and punishment. The less congruent or integrated our parents, the more we will have to deal with the results of their fragmentation later.

Another part of the confusion factor, however, springs from our position as "little people" dependent upon parents. Those "big people" were responsible for meeting many of our needs, but the course of daily living also meant that needs might be frustrated. Adult needs may need to come first, for example, or those of other children. Even with loving parents, a child's needs cannot always be met. During moments when interests clashed, if we expressed outrage or tried to fight back, we were likely to be overcome by angry parents who were bigger than we were. We thus learned quickly that we couldn't fight back. If we tried to flee, however, that didn't work either because that meant losing their love. The only available alternative was to freeze in confusion, then cut off the possibility of having these feelings again by deadening ourselves.

6. Existential crisis, despair

The hopelessness of this period can raise profound questions about the meaning of one's life. People may seriously question whether it makes sense to go on. Deep psychic pain can feel unbearable; life can seem hopeless.

When the emptiness seems unending, thoughts of suicide must be met with some form of inner or outer strength. One woman felt "saved" during this black period only because of her strong religious faith; another man who had no particular religion, clung to the memory of having debated suicide in a philosophical manner during college. Giving up had not been an option then, he remembered, so it wouldn't be acceptable now either.

In the face of this void and barrenness, the major task is to begin to connect with the spiritual level of self. This is our inner core or essence which has lain largely dormant since childhood. Before we contact that level, however, we need to "let go" of many emotional attachments and the trappings of our external sense of identity. An old definition of self must thoroughly die before the new takes hold.

7. Release of deep-seated emotional attachments

Feeling surrounded by death at every step is common during this stage, especially if we suffered abandonment from parents who were absent emotionally. Successfully coping with these feelings often depends on "letting go" of relationships that matter deeply. Once we do let go in an emotional sense, it is easier to see that these people didn't meet our needs. Our huge need for connection, love and safety, however, has obscured that truth. Dealing with such "unfinished business" frequently reveals itself during family crisis periods.

Betty's crisis involved trying "to go home again" to heal the damage from an unhappy childhood. Several years earlier her sister's out-of-wedlock child had brought the two sisters and their parents back together after years of arms-length talk. Naively, Betty hoped that the crisis would lead to more closeness among everyone. Instead, the dysfunctional roles from two generations of alcoholism were played out again in bold relief. The only variable this time was Betty's new awareness level. Despite her insight, however, she kept hoping that things might change. If she could grow, she thought, then they could too.

Betty's attempts to create better understanding, however, were met with bizarre responses. After being stung several times by her parents unchanged reactions, she felt hopeless that things might improve. Yet only in that hopelessness did she also see the "savior" role she had adopted. Now she could see that she was still trying to be "the hero" by making things right for everyone. Betty finally had to let go of the hope that these people could provide the love she needed. Now at least she knew what had formed her childhood.

Pursuing the inner journey means more than contacting new levels of self. It also means healing childhood memories. Naturally, if our parents are living, we "go back to the well" to try to make it turn out differently, or we find partners or friends who will play out family roles. In each case, we are trying to fill up the "hole in our soul" that arose when needs didn't get met before. We try desperately to get it "right" once more.

Only surrender to despair produces real change. After the agony of trying and trying again, we are forced back upon ourselves. When we accept the bitter disappointment that parents "should" have met our needs but didn't, we can more readily see that there is still self-love available. Such hard won truth includes the fact that inside each of us there is an internal core that is loving and good to begin with. Even as we let go the expectation that the parent or another family member will provide the desired response, however, often a substitute love object helps ease the transition. Letting go of our blood families means the opportunity to develop a "spiritual" family.

Whether or not we must face the fact that neither parent loved us satisfactorily, much of the work at this level involves release of childhood dependencies. As we let go these attachments, we learn some deeper lessons about our will and our ego. We need to learn, it seems, that having things come out *our* way is not the way life works. Instead, our will must become subservient to a higher will that we have barely begun to know.

8. Recovery of essence or our inner child

A higher will starts to come through as we release barriers and blockages. Below the surface of what may seem like unending heaviness there is "good news" stirring. If you do not keep a dream journal, where the signs of rebirth appear symbolically, or if you do not have some means to do emotional work with yourself, you may miss the outward signs of beginning to recontact your essence. By "essence" is meant an inner nature that defined us in childhood before we developed too much thinking and too many so-called civilized habits.

For example, Emily's therapy sessions included painful flashbacks as well as joyful mental pictures of a younger child. That little girl had been precocious, curious, loving, wise, sensual, mischievous and playful. Regaining a sense of that child amounted to more than recovering a lost past. In a still fragile way those pictures were saying something about her as an adult. Despite these reassurances, however, there were only fleeting glimpses that a more solid "self" was forming beneath the surface. Every small advance seemed followed by a pull back into confusion and molasses. Only the flashback pictures of that inner child indicated that an important self-definition process was slowly taking hold, this time from the inside out.

9. Personal/universal understanding and identification

Author Anais Nin, known for her diaries and her championship of women, wrote about the inner journey in a way that showed she was way ahead of her time *(A Woman Speaks)*. Nin suggested that inevitably "the personal journey leads us to the universal." She meant that all of us have been affected by certain major issues of our time; the more deeply we go into ourselves, the more we understand this common bond. Ironically, in the depths of our despair, we discover that our private trauma parallels that of others; we are part of the unfolding human drama.

Awareness that we are not alone in our pain comes often during grief workshops such as those done by the Kubler-Ross organization. Initially, each person comes to the workshop encased in their own private story of pain. As the week continues, trauma after trauma unfolds. The story of a holocaust survivor provides a dramatic example. About midweek, he began to share memories from the concentration camps, crying out in anguish, not only for himself, but also for "his people," the exterminated Jews who had lost family members in the gas chambers and death camps. He described horrible crimes. Huge tears rolled down his craggy cheeks; he wrapped his arms around himself to contain the sobs; he rocked back and forth in grief. At first the man couldn't believe that anyone else could relate to his sorrow; nothing could be worse than this unfathomable pain, he thought. As various participants responded to him with silent tears, a few words or merely a heartfelt look, however, slowly he realized that some of them *did* understand this very hellish anguish.

The lesson in such a group setting is that most people suffer grief about something. Whether the cause is loss of a parent, abuse, death of a child, being an AIDS victim, suicide, Vietnam horror or being a crime victim, the common denominator is unbearable suffering. Keeping it locked inside poisons us, but when we dare to feel it and share it, we find healing and community with others.

Another way to become aware of our identification with the universal condition is to examine our dreams. Some may be surprisingly impersonal. Jerry recalled, for example, one dream that occurred when he wasn't dealing with any particular relationship. The material seemed surprising; it was about what happened when men took care of women, as in the traditional male/female pattern of man as breadwinner and woman as homemaker. The dream image was of women choking on food that had been fed to them by men. The punch line was that "the food got stuck in their throats while the man looked elsewhere for others to fuck." The dream was a commentary about how dependency chokes people from growing, and that men go elsewhere for sexual satisfaction when saddled with an emotional child.

Glenda's dream occurred shortly after she discovered some strong abuse from her brother. The impersonal dream, however, depicted her standing in a courtroom, screaming against the rules that had been set up by men. A second scene featured men acting silly and irresponsible. She felt that both images reflected more than her personal outrage; in some way they depicted societal situations and a set of patriarchal rules devised without women's participation. Both Glenda and Jerry had experienced some universal dream material. His was about female dependency and hers was about male dominance, reflecting the fact that many of us struggle to overcome the weight of centuries within our psyches.

The most compelling identification with the universal, however, can come from daily events that we now see with "new eyes" and a heightened sensitivity. During this stage in my process, I suddenly was aware everywhere of how often women suffer put downs, from women as much as men. I felt unbearably sad when I saw that, as though I was carrying the weight of the pain of all women; I felt men's sorrow too, for they also have been wounded by unbalanced feminine/masculine forces. Both my body and my soul ached with weariness at times, as though I could hardly take one more step to keep going. Such strong identification with the suffering of humanity is characteristic at this stage. We truly take on the cares of the world for a while.

10. Images of birth, prebirth, past-life, etc.

In addition to the range of unusual visions and sensations reported by participants in the Grof workshops, other therapists, especially rebirthers, verify the ability of their clients to access images of birth and prebirth. Most people are startled to find that they can return to these memories, but those who are able to check them against actual circumstances find them amazingly accurate.

Often the birth process was difficult in some way so that reliving it seems to clear up significant issues. One man, now a minister, discovered through a rebirthing session that his twin had died at birth. His mother had never shared this information, perhaps because she had not come to terms with the grief herself. Once David verified the facts, however, a huge sense of loss and guilt was lifted. The false guilt had come from the awareness that he had been the twin who lived; the loss was similar to that felt by any twin who loses their sibling.

Besides reliving one's birth, there may be the mysterious ability to recall fetal or embryonic experiences as well. One woman, for example, felt she knew the emotional atmosphere that had surrounded her parent's lovemaking when she was conceived. At first she couldn't believe she could know this, yet the awareness was crystal clear. Her father had considered his need for a woman a weakness, so their act of love had been anything but a celebration. Once the daughter accepted this recollection as valid, she realized it meant starting life at the embryo level through a veil of shame and guilt.

The ability to remember past lives, especially if there was something traumatic about it, is another unexplainable phenomena that can occur. Hollywood star Shirley MacLaine dramatized this aspect of spiritual work in her popular book, *Dancing In The Light*. The therapist who helped MacLaine uncover past life memories was Chris Griscom who now runs The Light Institute in Galisteo, New Mexico. Griscom's healing work focuses on helping people clear their emotional bodies, an aspect that she believes is encrusted with layers of past life and childhood memories.

11. Sensations/images of rebirth

After months of feeling as though I was struggling for my life, breakthrough came one day as I was working on mother-related issues. While lying on the therapy table, I was plunged into the vacuum of a black hole; then I seemed to fall through chasms of enormous pain. On the other side of that terror-filled vacuum, however, was the mental image of my baby self in a tall version, walking joyfully on mother's stomach. Obviously, my actual birth had not been this way. With this breakthrough, however, I knew I had broken the parental spell. Symbolically, I could walk on my own now.

Another woman was able to identify a nine month process of almost unbearable pain before she broke through a similar barrier. Her rapture about this transition was so strong that she decided to change her name. The old identity was no longer sufficient for her expanded sense of self.

The sense of rebirth at the end of this stage comes primarily from contacting the underlying core of essence, our inner child or our higher self.

Such a core or center has always been there, but it has been repressed. The degree of damage to that inner child depends upon the nature of your parenting and how sensitively you reacted, but even so-called healthy families were places where essence was denied. Society so far has been conducted at the level of acquired personality rather than essence, so most of us must go through a process of recovering what was there in the first place.

Another aspect to rebirth, however, is that this core of essence and our higher self must be developed in mature ways during middle age. In our 20s and 30s we are building careers, finding mates and creating families. All of these help us know in an outer sense who we are. During Tension/Confusion/Conflict, however, we begin to really break through the barrier of an externally defined self. At this stage we begin to know what it means to function beyond our egocentric shell.

Many authors refer to this process as ego death. This does *not* mean that we must kill off this part of ourselves or negate it as part of our psychic structure, but rather that we must let go the tight grip on the ego as the only way to define ourselves. When we have the courage to do the work of this level, we discover a deeper realm of reality, a part of self that eventually becomes the master. The ego then becomes subservient to this higher self; it can support and add to one's life without being dominant as before.

12. Learning to trust bodily wisdom; allowing and surrender

Much of the work at this level has to do with unfreezing our body. Especially if we seek body work therapy, such as acupressure or massage, we are likely to wake up areas numbed during childhood. As stored pain is released, the effect is to increasingly trust the wisdom of the body. If you are physically hurting, for example, you may need to pay attention to some internal conflict. Your body will also tell you simple things, such as when you need sleep, food, exercise or work, at a pace in tune with your own rhythm and needs rather than those of the clock. During times when you might not know what to do next, you can tune into yourself physically and intuitively for next directions. We cannot use the body in such a way, however, unless it has become clear of the interfering "noise" of frozen pain.

As we progressively learn to trust the body/mind connection, we also begin to trust the universe more. We can relax and flow with life rather than fight it. The reason for no longer needing to control things is that contact with an internal self lessens the need for security from external measures. This may be the beginning of a true sense of faith. Another way to explain what has happened is that we learn, through the countless repetitions of "letting go," that holding on to the way we think things "should" go does not work. Behind the painful episodes of being forced to continually release attachments, is the important ability to surrender to the moment. Perhaps it is human nature to resist change and to avoid pain, yet the lessons of this particular passage show us that we make faster progress when we "allow" life to happen. Knowing when to trust, surrender and let things unfold in their own way are vital benefits from this stage.

COPING STRATEGIES
1. Allow time for "clearing;" nurture yourself

Nancy and Glenda used to joke about which one had the heating pad turned on that weekend. They were referring to the need to nurse sore spots after a therapy session. If you have moved through a major blockage it is important to be kind to yourself while the negative residues move through the body. Doing strenuous emotional work can give us the sense of being "cleared." Such clearing is both a physical and mental awareness that the previous conflict is gone; one feels lighter, more buoyant, no longer weighed down by oppressive feelings or pain. The rigor of the work, however, can be exhausting. Pampering yourself and taking it easy are advisable. Nancy felt that the sense of clearing, then movement or healing, usually occurred within 36 hours of the actual physical release. During that 36 hours she was especially vulnerable; she needed additional rest and could not face demanding social situations.

2. Seek medical help if you need it

The stress given to the presence of physical aches and pains as "normal" during this stage should not be misconstrued. There may, in other words, be reason to seek medical help along with doing the emotional clearing work. Each person must judge for themselves.

3. Don't give up! Allow the sadness to persist without beating yourself up about not feeling better

Know that the pain and emptiness will lessen and eventually pass. When despair seems unending or unbearable, wait a little longer. And, if all you can do is cry or feel blue, then just accept this as an enormously sad period without making further demands on yourself. Eventually the heaviness lifts if you keep working with the process. Above all, reach out for help and comfort if you are truly desperate; if the person doesn't respond at all or does so unsatisfactorily, reach again. You will find the right person if you just don't give up.

4. Try to remember that "letting go" is of primary importance

What does it mean to "let go?" It's a difficult concept to describe, yet learning that we must do it in large and small ways is a constant lesson. "Letting go" often involves allowing ourselves to grieve deeply for what cannot be; sometimes it means feeling the emotions that surround a person or event rather than denying them. When we can feel the feelings, without labeling or judging them as good or bad, there is almost a miraculous sense that they then pass through us. And every time we can release pain, expectations or attachments, we feel lighter and clearer afterwards, as though a fresh wind is blowing through our life.

The "letting go" process can also be accompanied by great moments of understanding and insight. David, for example, realized with the help of intense breathwork therapy, that he had been severely abused as a child. Previously the memories of these events had been hidden in his unconscious. Dredging them up was anything but fun, but at least he knew now what his stepmother had done. Finding these skeletons also increased his confidence about being a good parent himself. As painful as it may be to dredge up memories, there is great consolation in reliving personal horrors. Such knowledge gives meaning and purpose to an individual life. When we understand the forces and events that formed us, we build a new, internal sense of identity, not one based upon education, money or status. The irony of knowing yourself at deep levels in terms of the past is that you can then put the past aside. Our personal history becomes part of our anchor. The need to dwell on it, however, virtually disappears as it becomes a platform for living more fully in the present.

5. Accept your vulnerability

As we work issues through in-depth, we are forced to become aware of our own fragile nature, especially the vulnerability we had as children. Out of such new self-respect also grows a deeper compassion for others. If we have fully cried for ourselves, we can empathize better with others.

While we are getting in touch with this vulnerable past, it is common to feel especially sensitive to the everyday issues that trigger old hurts. Work conditions, for example, can mirror childhood conditions. Bosses or colleagues can be uncannily like family members. Especially when we become aware of the patriarchy and its abuse, we can see and feel its effects everywhere. One woman executive feared she might lose control of herself while on the job at a paper products company. "Men just don't listen," she screamed inside to herself. "They don't even see us; they're unconscious!" For a while each work encounter was loaded with past hurts as well as present behavior that felt unjust. Her newfound awareness made her flinch like a wounded animal.

Eventually she found the strength to mount an effective protest. She confronted the men in her team when they didn't listen; she refused to train another man who would then be promoted over her head. She asked for a salary increase. In the meantime, being kind to herself by merely accepting this vulnerable state was helpful. Others also report being overly sensitive for a time to the suffering in the world at large. They can hardly stand to watch news programs or read the papers because daily events seem so full of tragedy; life is already unbearable at this stage, and they can't stand to see or hear any more.

6. Find safe places and methods to rage out the rage, but give parents a break

It is crucial to feel the depths of your feelings, including all the terror, rage and anger at parents or others that may be locked inside. We need safe places and safe ways to do that, however. Seldom should the clearing be done in the physical presence of the perpetrators themselves. Later, when the venting has spent itself, you may need to say "NO" to them, to do various things that change the patterns of your relationship. You may also need to write letters that never get sent or at least to weigh the consequences before you act.

Sometimes we need to have our say. One fateful interchange between a woman and her father, for example, was the letter she sent that told him off in no uncertain terms. It was a letter that neither parent would forgive, yet for Cecilia it was an important confrontation. At issue was her self-worth and the ability to take truly adult risks. The father had repeatedly misinterpreted his daughter's communications; his rigidity was impenetrable. Cecilia realized that saying "NO" was long overdue. She decided that taking a stand with him was vital; if the purpose had been only to vent her anger, the decision might have been to write the letter and throw it out.

Instead, the letter symbolized her emancipation from years of verbal assaults; it also successfully called a halt to the father's habit of dumping his anger about other family members onto her. The risk, of course, was that he would stop speaking to her about anything; that did happen. As sad as that outcome was, Cecilia never again feared in quite the same ways the loss of love and approval from male authority figures that has been built into our culture.

How we handle communications during these intense years is important. When in doubt, weigh situations carefully. Consider options and consequences; ask for suggestions from others, then do what you need to do to best take care of yourself.

The prescription to "give parents a break," however, means to consider the difference in the forces that formed you versus them. It is helpful to realize, for example, that dysfunctional families have been the norm rather than the exception in recent centuries. The truth is that most of us have been the product of conditional love because society has not been ready to function at higher levels. Most of us were raised with the suppression of our childhood essence. To some extent, socialization itself requires that we be denied these "natural" expressions of self. Limits and boundaries must be imposed by parents as we grow up. Yet the patriarchy itself has been a time when parental needs dominated the scene. Rights of children have seldom been considered. Those who have been deeply violated by these conditions must protest in order to save ourselves. At the same time, it is unfair to blame and punish our unknowing parents. Rather, we need to grieve.

Someday in the future, when people have thrown off the damaging effects of the patriarchy, the whole business of parenting will be different.

Then parents will be more capable of both unconditional love and effective limit setting. In the meantime, however, the break in history that characterizes current times is hard on both parents and children. Once the raging is done, it is helpful to remember that those parents were deeply affected by the Depression and two World Wars. Providing a higher economic standard was primary in their lives. Psychological growth of the kind now occurring to many was unavailable to them.

7. Don't underestimate the work of this stage, nor the potential need for outside support and help

Tension/Confusion/Conflict appears to span much of the critical fourth year. Here the earlier seeds of rebirth either deepen and ripen or else they scatter into a psychic death that creates bitterness and disappointment. To make this transition, we must find the support to work deeply and to connect with a new level of self. Indeed, resolution of the hopelessness and sense of death that is common seems dependent upon connection to our spiritual source.

This particular phase of the inner journey represents a kind of growth that is still mostly underestimated and misunderstood in society. Because we lack clear understandings of the process, some of the symptoms of this stage can mean serious misdiagnosis and mistreatment. Some of the more bizarre images that may be experienced, for example, do not mean one is insane although they are commonly interpreted that way; similarly, it may be "natural" to have some suicidal thoughts when death of the ego is required. In a very real sense we must repeatedly die to ourselves in order to live again. But persistent suicidal thoughts or actual attempts are serious indeed. Instead of turning to drug sedation or emotional rescue, however, people need to know that there will be an end to their psychic pain. They need to know how "normal" are the abnormal symptoms of this stage and how heroic is the inner work required. The truth is that many of us may need a "midwife," shaman, therapist or guide to successfully bridge this rocky passage.

5

Bottoming Out:

Falling Apart and Rejoicing

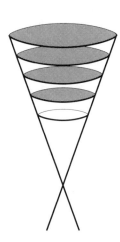

Her father's condition was worsening. A diagnosis of congestive heart failure meant death was near. As preposterous as it sounded, Cindy knew she would be blamed. Her brother had already been accused of making him sick. Fear of her parent's reactions became so strong that she considered cancelling the trip. She shuddered physically in anticipation. How could she hold herself together for the week at home? Reinforcement came from an extra therapy session. Yes, Cindy was paranoid, but not without reason either. The fears that went back to childhood were resurfacing now with a vengeance. She felt momentarily powerless to push them back.

Although this stage requires fewer "letting go" episodes, it can contain some of the most intense emotions of the entire cycle. Paranoia or rage are not uncommon; consequently, both therapist and friends can make a huge difference in coping. Another hallmark is the need to acknowledge our grief about not having received the love we needed. Considerable pain has already preceded this stage, yet here we reach the bottom of our sadness or hurt. Uncontrollable crying is often the case. After such brief episodes, however, when "falling apart" seems called for, considerable clearing can occur, often accompanied by moments of great meaning, lightness or freedom. Here is where we can move beyond the personal hurts (to the transpersonal) as well as say "NO" to abusive patterns.

IDENTIFYING CHARACTERISTICS

1. Healing of memories continues; rapid breakthroughs, faster cycling

Now the bad days were outnumbered by good ones. In therapy sessions, the flashbacks to childhood continued, but these were often followed during the same session by breakthroughs. By breakthrough I mean that clearing and resolution occurred during the session rather than afterwards. If I had surfaced another painful episode about my father, for example, often the crying spell was followed immediately by uproarious laughter or freeing release. No longer did I spend time in between sessions in prolonged agony; the sense of being so horribly stuck was absent.

Increasingly the therapist employed an "imaging" technique that took advantage of the previous work we'd done. As the hurtful incidents were raised to consciousness through his gentle touch, he suggested I call upon my "other" self to be available for the wounded child, teenager or woman. This "double" self merely held or comforted the hurting person in my mind's eye. Such imaging provided the unconditional love and nurturing to heal that particular memory. Being able to picture myself in this dual way was a reparenting process that employed the new part of self that had emerged in prior work. Each time I contacted this totally nonjudgmental, loving center, I felt healed; within 24 hours I was usually contemplating new work ideas or personal goals. I was no longer stuck.

2. Increased inner peace, freedom, lightness, joy, safety

As the flashbacks continued, more and more inner peace took hold. The sessions themselves often ended with a burst of energy and joy. It was as though I had learned how to die repeatedly to myself on that acupressure table; each time I did, the sense of self that is beyond ego became more anchored. Consequently, I felt "safe" for the first time in my life. Touching this core of inner solidity over and over again produced a sense of having arrived somewhere secure at last.

As the inner peace was strengthened, daily living held new aliveness. Small things, such as wearing a warm bathrobe or watching the dance of a crackling fire, took on enhanced pleasure. The simplest activities felt joyful; tastes, sights and sounds provided immense satisfaction about merely being alive.

3. Sense of impending doom

Underneath this growing sense of abundance, however, lay a ledge of sadness. Without knowing what it was or why, I had a disturbing foreboding about the future. Somewhere out there was a precipice of unknown origin and outcome.

Stanislav Grof suggests that this feeling of impending catastrophe is related to the experience of ego death itself (Grof, 1988, p. 30). To go through such death would naturally evoke fears and a sense of dread. Actually, the experience of multiple deaths would be a more accurate way to describe what actually happens, for we must repeatedly dip into the unconscious to complete the process. Part of the difficulty in describing the sensation is that feelings of abundance exist alongside the foreboding.

4. Experiences of connection, fusion, "oneness"

David used to try, unsuccessfully, to share how he felt when he was jogging through the Colorado countryside; merging with the trees and the birds was part of a thrill that went beyond words. Usually he sounded crazy to others when he tried to explain. Susan also had merging feelings; hers were with people on city streets or with animals. Her sense of fusion included prolonged moments when she and another person were all one and the same. The knowing looks she exchanged with neighbor's pets convinced her they had communicated without words. Both David and Susan reported a heightened sense of pleasure during these moments, as though one smiles inwardly about having penetrated a cosmic secret. There is strong awareness of being connected to the universe at such times; such fusions are concrete evidence of what the mystics call the "oneness of things."

Other mystical or paranormal experiences that break through ordinary knowledge of space/time limitations cover an extraordinary range of psychic phenomena, from identification with plants or rocks to contacts with the dead to encounters with spirit guides. Both wrathful and blissful deities can be experienced. Grof's *The Adventure of Self-Discovery* contains one of the most comprehensive discussions of these wide-ranging phenomena. Some 60% of the population claims such experiences, yet talking about them remains difficult in a culture that does not yet accept the mystic or the mysterious.

5. Deepened sense of meaning, identification, revelations

As the healing continued, my dips into the past increasingly brought more global insights about what lay below the wounds. Episodes felt less personal and more related to broader psycho/social factors. Feminine/masculine imbalance was the pervasive theme of so much that needed healing in my background as well as my friends. Whether the mother or father had been alcoholic, whether either parent had been dominant or weak, the underlying patterns were still the same; there were countless examples of parents who had not been whole people.

Did any truly healthy families exist? Unfortunately, I concluded that all past marriages involved a woman and a man who each played out half the human equation rather then uniting the inner feminine/masculine. As I listened to others' stories, I heard a wide ranging of examples, from the controlling mother to the passive woman, from the homosexual father to the rigid patriarch. Alcoholism was unbelievably common. However the aberrations had played themselves out, it was apparent that both past and present generations were victims of prescribed, stereotypical roles. Intimacy and wholeness had been absent.

As I came to terms with my underlying issues, I realized how young the world was in its knowledge of healthy relationships and love. So much of what people are grieving has to do with failed relationships in general. The words of a wise Episcopal priest came to mind. He said years ago that Christianity had never yet really had a chance in the world. Now I could see why. Christianity preaches "brotherly love," yet it has taken us nearly 2000 years to be ready to know how to love ourselves from an inner state. And only when we love ourselves can we love another.

As I saw deeper meaning in things, even the presence of evil was easier to accept. Everywhere I looked, I could see how good things emerged from the seeming bad. Marsha, for example, who portrayed her father as cruel, selfish, authoritarian and unyielding, had developed much of her character as a result of his actions. His evil was the "dark side" that he had never raised to consciousness. For her, however, his destructive flaws had ultimately been the impetus for growth. Another man who had suffered molestation by his mother went on to incorporate innovative healing practices in his therapy practice.

Several weekends during this period were filled with dramatic revelations. My emotions ranged from the tears of deep sadness to the relief of knowing wisdom. Somewhere at the bottom of the grief was a profound respect, even a deep gratitude for this heroic journey. Certainly the worst parts of the journey had pushed me to the limits, but the battle was being won. I could see so plainly now that without the wounds, I would have never found this depth; without the pain, I would have never found my self.

As Elisabeth Kubler-Ross says, "It is the windstorms of life that make us who we are." Now I could accept that the bad, unpleasant, hurtful or so-called "wrong" things in life were only the "windstorms that deepened the caverns." There was, indeed, a wisdom and goodness to life that could be respected if we can just see below the surface.

6. Acceptance of one's spiritual nature

In common usage, the term "spiritual" is *not* synonymous with "religious." To be religious generally means to participate in formal church membership and practices, whereas to be spiritual implies an outlook on life that comes from inner experience. Most notable about a spiritual outlook is a reverence for life, an appreciation for one's unique purpose and an acceptance that there are powers greater than oneself.

During Fear/Guilt/Grief, we accept our spiritual nature with new humility and gratitude; we have been brought to our knees often enough to know that there are larger powers at work. A combination of events, however, adds up to the development of a spiritual outlook. These include mystical or paranormal experiences that cannot be rationally explained, awareness of a new level of self and a growing appreciation for larger meanings.

Many people at this point begin to look for a new way to deepen this spiritual outlook by returning to formal religion or finding a new form. Those who left organized religion in earlier years may search for new ways to celebrate. They often cannot go back to the old structures. After the rigor and rewards of inner growth, they seek an atmosphere and an ideology that is considerably broader than that provided by many churches. Still others may return to church with a totally new outlook, or they will make an abrupt change to a different denomination.

7. Paranoia, panic, terror, rage

At this level we are working with the feelings suppressed in the *emotional defense layer*. As Alexander Lowen points out, "What lies here is the rage, panic, terror, despair, sadness and pain residing closest to our central core" (Lowen, 1975, p. 120). Accordingly, as we allow these emotions to surface, we can be struck with some of the most intense but shortest-lived reactions of the journey. Fortunately, the fact that we have also begun to tap into our core essence helps us undertake this aspect.

Cindy, the woman who feared going home to face her dying father and the possibility of parental blame, is an example of intense fear and paranoia. Her fears were not groundless; they were based in accurate perceptions of family dynamics. The potential threat this posed to Cindy, however, was blown way out of proportion. The panicky feelings she experienced accorded her parents far more power than they actually possessed. Cindy, of course, was reacting to this adult situation from her childhood state. It took on paranoid tones because she was inwardly reliving that childhood. At the same time she was outwardly engaging her family as an adult.

Cindy was currently doing the emotional work that took her back to infancy. During those early months of life, she likely experienced fear that was never expressed. Parents left her alone, let her cry too much, didn't feed her on demand or punished her without good reason. Imagine the terror for a child, even in a family where needs were largely met. Children repress these times of abandonment, punishment and emptiness. Their inner world is one of terror about an unfriendly and menacing place, but this is masked in order to live in the real world (Nichols, 1986, p. 140). At this stage of midlife growth, we reexperience those feelings.

Our fears at those tender ages may very well have been unfounded; they may have been the product of being little in a world of big people. On the other hand, the fears may be grounded in stark reality; many parents were unable to provide the emotional support a child needs; many were decidedly abusive in emotional as well as physical and sexual ways. Regardless of the source of our fears or their severity, we didn't imagine them. They were real. Daring to make that original terror conscious is part of deep inner change.

8. Falling apart

David's friend, Robert, had called him from the office. He was cancelling his afternoon appointments. Could he meet David for the afternoon at the old farmhouse? The call sounded urgent, and it was. During that wintry afternoon, with a roaring fire, several glasses of wine and quarts of herbal tea, Robert broke down. His grief was mainly about his father, who had died when he was nine. Robert's halting words about this enormous sadness swiftly turned into sobs; David held him and poured more tea. Wave after wave of despair came tumbling out. David said little; his own stepmother had been the source of so much of his own pain. He knew that what mattered most was to just be there while his friend cried it out.

Later that afternoon the two men talked quietly, hopefully about life. Robert was eager now to share this episode with his wife. He felt strangely lighthearted. In fact, he felt surrounded by light as he traveled back to the city. David's care and comfort had provided a safety valve; just his being there had provided some boundaries and some solace for uncontrollable grief, a torrent that had emerged suddenly, without warning. Robert was figuratively "letting go of father" during those hours, but he was also letting go of his fears and sadness about dependency in general.

The sense of "falling apart" at this stage reflects the separation from love objects that is essential if we are to become grounded in a new level of self. Uncontrollable sobbing is not uncommon, as are "crying jags" that leave us wondering whether we can get through the week. It is as though the helpless child that we once were knows again that the "togetherness" of the womb can never be repeated. Thus, we are alone and lonely, unable, momentarily, to be comforted. The sobbing or grieving tends to have a hopeless quality, yet it immediately lifts if we allow it to run its course.

9. Strengthened sense of self; finding the transpersonal

One of the most profound lessons from encountering these darkest moments is that we can actually "fall apart" without suffering harm. Falling apart, in fact, turns out to be healing. At the bottom of that abyss, we find the core or essential self. Indeed, the only way through this stage is to allow the pain to be expressed. Allowing our worst fears to be felt, or admitting our darkest sins, has the effect of what some people call "grace."

Below the despair, terror, guilt or shame, we can then "see" the meaning of a particular event. Perhaps we can even see the meaning of our life in general. When we can touch the core of self-love that is in us, when we can accept all of our experience and forgive that, a sense of release and compassion floods the being. A sense of thanksgiving for all the heartaches we've suffered is common. You begin to feel increasingly that there has been nothing personal in this at all; indeed, suffering and struggle is, in fact, the necessary lot of humanity in general.

This sense of being beyond the personal is where the term "transpersonal" comes in. Below the level of personal hurts and individual concerns there is a deep, loving center that exists beyond such events. Each of us undergoes trials to find that core; each of us must find the meaning in our particular story.

10. Surrender; change in perception; healthy resignation

Despite the fact that you feel less outer suffering than before at this stage (except for certain intense moments or hours), it is common to go through incident after incident of learning continually that you must surrender to larger forces. Increasingly, we recognize that we cannot control the outcome of external events. We eventually give up trying to make it turn out "our way."

Another "giving up" can be the roles we played in our families and are still repeating in various ways. This includes being overly responsible now for situations because you played the "hero" or some other role in a family affected by alcoholism. One of my clients was a prime example. One day the blame and anger in their high-powered management team became focused on me after a team-building session. Paranoia struck, almost immobilizing me, when I realized afterwards that the CEO wasn't going to look at his unconscious behavior. The conflicts within the man at the top were being played out in the management team. This time I was the scapegoat. Previously it had been one or another of the vice-presidents.

Before the meeting ended, I had tangibly absorbed their anger. For hours afterwards, the supposed statements they might hurl at me in the future ran through my head. In response, I prepared obsessive counter-arguments. After the initial wave of fear had passed, I regained my senses. I realized that I didn't need to solve their problems. Few of the men had been genuinely interested in looking at their behavior; now I could see the futility of our efforts. I was sick and tired of being set up to take the blame; no longer did I need to accept the burden of making it "come out right." That was false guilt and I could put it aside.

As I looked anew at this situation with sudden detachment, I could see how often other work blockages had arisen from unconscious triggers. This CEO was undoubtedly mirroring conflicts I still had about my father, for example. Our communication would inevitably be tainted because I was still struggling to be free of this "unfinished business." Similarly, the men's buried conflicts with mothers or sisters might get played out with me. We were all unwitting partners in a tangled, hidden web of issues that went way back in the collective unconscious of history.

11. Ability to say "NO" to abusive patterns

Besides surrendering in healthy resignation to problems you cannot solve and situations you cannot change, another likely event at this stage is a new-found ability to say "NO" to abusive patterns. Cindy's experience *after* she conquered her paranoia about going home is a good example. As she walked into the house, her fears escalated again. Her father ranted and raved for over an hour that evening, about everything from hospital bills, to the in-laws, to the accusation that her brother's behavior as a teenager had caused his illness.

Initially Cindy felt shaken by the familiar diatribe. She excused herself and took a brief walk in order to collect her thoughts. When she returned, Cindy reacted in a manner her parents had never seen before. She sat down squarely in front of her father and told him bluntly she would listen to no more accusations. When he protested, trying to perpetuate the complaints, Cindy interrupted and said "NO" again. As he looked up in surprise, Cindy left the room, signalling that she would not participate. Several days later she again exercised her firmness; as her father attempted to reopen the subject, Cindy said quietly that she would get on the plane if he continued. He retreated meekly to his newspaper.

Another example of saying "NO," combined with the extreme reactions of this stage, was my reaction to a broken engagement. I felt fooled and foolish when the man cancelled our wedding plans and ran off like a scared rabbit. Besides feeling publicly embarrassed, I was also enraged. Appearing foolish before others was one of my last, uncovered fears. The anger was so strong that I felt capable of physical assault. That awareness alone was a shock. Fortunately, I had the sense not to act on the feelings.

Later, in the therapy session that followed, I experienced searing, bottomless pain. How could I bear one more hurtful episode at this vulnerable stage? For part of that hour I was truly devastated. This time, however, I also found the will to say "NO" to such cycles. Clearly, I had had enough pain, enough refusals, enough abandonment. Something about this desperation made me feel as though I could protect myself in the future.

Taking place beneath that hurtful incident, was the maturation of a strengthened authentic self. Like the alcoholic who may need to hit bottom before he/she starts to get well, so too with addictive emotional patterns. In this case my romance addiction had played itself out. I had had enough, and I vowed that I would learn how to take care of myself in the future. (Taking care of myself might mean proceeding much more slowly before I trusted completely enough to give away my heart.)

When we finally reach the limits of playing out these repetitive, harmful patterns, we develop new strength about making different choices. Another way of saying this is that we are no longer "at the affect" of other people; we can stop reacting personally to many situations. We need no longer accept the guilt that others may want us to have in order to control our behavior. We no longer get caught so easily in the escalating dynamics of unhealthy communication. Now it is possible to see things for what they are, then do what is required to take care of ourselves without judging others. Such inner strength, based upon awareness of our boundaries and limits, creates trust that *struggle* need not be a way of learning lessons in the future. Some people would say that karma ends here.

12. Creativity appears; outer interest, new directions beckon

New hope graced Mark's days as his creativity bloomed. The divorce dragged on and on, with his wife making unreasonable, revengeful demands. The separation from his teenage children was agonizing, but he felt hopeful about several other things. One was a new girlfriend; another was his career shift. Not too long ago the future had looked so bleak that he wondered if life was worth living.

Mark's career interests were shifting dramatically from engineering to psychology. He was in the process of applying for graduate school in counseling. His girlfriend was considering moving with him to Colorado if he got accepted. Mark's switch was the result of many years of frustration in research environments. Politics and back-stabbing dominated the companies where he'd worked, rather than cooperation and teamwork. The new career interest, however, was also the result of his recent personal search. A combination of therapy, men's group work and his own voracious appetite for self-knowledge had led him to Jungian and transpersonal psychology. Mark knew he had further work to do, but he was pretty sure he had survived the worst tests. He was more than ready to start integrating his experience with academic knowledge. Within several years he would be ready to counsel and teach others.

While it is a mistake to think at this stage that one is "finished" or beyond pain, there is nonetheless a distinct feeling that one is above the raging storm. In the future we will be more able to get our needs met from a basis of fullness rather than deficiency. At last we are much freer to pursue new discoveries without being laden with "baggage."

COPING STRATEGIES
1. Do reach for help or comfort from someone who understands

Usually the moments of paranoia, panic, rage or "falling apart" are not lengthy ones; some dissipate within several hours. Others, however, may require several days and the help of someone else. When extreme reactions occur, it may be important to be with someone, whether that is a friend or a therapist. The person need not necessarily be skilled about "doing the right thing" so much as someone who is involved in their own inner work and able to provide support. This is because someone who has *not* embarked upon the journey will be pushed into panic themselves by the depths of your pain. The primary concern is to be with someone who can express unconditional love. You don't need solutions or even counseling so much as someone who can let you dissolve without doing much of anything except *be there* in a nonjudgmental, supportive way.

My ex-fiance, for example, had already begun his emotional departure from our relationship when I fell apart one evening. Our friendship and his high self-awareness, however, meant that he was able to comfort me for several hours. The source of my pain was not him, but my family. As my unbroken sobs rolled out, he held me in his arms as he would a child. I couldn't seem to stop crying, although the cause of it all was muddy. A profound sense of abandonment swept through me in rippling waves. Never before had I allowed myself to come unglued so completely. Later, he fed me chicken soup and put me gently to bed, as though I was a baby. I fell asleep immediately in exhausted relief. Later I realized that I had been grieving the loss of some sort of primal mother bond.

2. Don't expect some experiences to make sense

Some experiences during Fear/Guilt/Grief are simply beyond words. Body work can be especially effective in raising unusual sensations. Perhaps they had their origin in infancy before we had words, or they may stem from the inner regions of the psyche that are formless. Making sense of them isn't nearly as important as purging their pain from our systems.

3. Avoid seeking the sensational for sensation's sake

Some of the byproducts of work at this stage, such as encounters with mystical spirits, surrealistic light, past-life regressions, out-of-body travel or merging with others, can be understood as experiences transcending the normal limits of the ego boundaries. Such episodes take us into a dimension beyond ordinary reality. We feel mystical and mystified about them because they are not explainable in terms of everyday consciousness. Their occurrence, however, is usually unforgettable. Indeed, these profound experiences are often the ones that change our lives.

However frightened, awed or pleased we may be about such events, it is a mistake to expect them or to seek them as ends in themselves. One new age proponent, for example, was so determined to have an out-of-body experience that he made himself miserable because he couldn't. He was also arrogantly focused on the wrong goal. The danger in emphasizing these events too much is that they become faddish hopes, even cultist movements. I also suggest that you use some discretion when you share your experiences. Bragging about mystical episodes can become just another way to say you're better than others.

Some useful perspective about these so-called "supernatural" events is offered by Doug Boyd, author of *Rolling Thunder,* an account of his apprenticeship with a medicine man. Boyd said in a 1988 class on "Personal Power", "No other culture except ours has been so *out* of touch with their own natural powers." In other words, what we now perceive as paranormal, mystical and supernatural was previously accepted as part of the natural order. Other cultures, such as Native American Indians or Aboriginal, have never had difficulty accepting such events as living proof of their connection with the universe. Our drive to become conscious, rational and scientific has unfortunately relegated such beliefs to the category of superstition and unprovable nonsense. Now, however, we live in times when it is possible to go above ordinary consciousness to a kind of super-consciousness that is beyond scientific proof. Within the next decade or two, science and psychology will develop plausible explanations of these phenomena. Then we will be able once again to move in and out of spirit at will.

4. Trust that you will receive whatever you need

Some people have near-death experiences; some people experience their past lives, while others do not. The important thing is that we will each be given whatever we need for healing, meaning and growth. Beware, however, of jumping on the bandwagon of anything, whether that be crystal healing, channeling or past-life regressions. Whatever was right for Shirley MacLaine is not necessarily right for you. MacLaine has come to symbolize the flakier approaches to inner growth, although she did us a service by publicizing out-of-body experiences, channeling, extra-terrestrial visits and the spiritual journey in general.

Each of us is a unique human with widely differing backgrounds and potential. Whatever we need for our healing, whatever we need to establish meaning in our lives, and whatever we need to unfold our talent, will be provided if we have the courage to seek and become aware. The bounty of what we do find constitutes both our personal lessons and a potential gift to others. Those who uncover severe abuse, for example, are often the best equipped to turn around and help others through their healing. Only in our new-found compassion and creativity does it become apparent that we can live out the idea of "the wounded healer." This is Henri Nouwen's term for a state of mind that goes beyond counseling or ministering. Nouwen meant that only when we become aware of our own wounds do we find the true capacity to minister to others.

5. Congratulate yourself for "facing the lion"

As we dare to face the "lion" of our fears, grief and guilt, we can be healed of the wounds that produced them. By having the courage to go deeply inward and to feel with such intensity, we purge ourselves of negative emotions. This, in turn, means that we can transcend them.

Finally Marsha accepted, for example, that her father would never change. He had simply done the best that he could with his limitations. Later, after her own healing had progressed substantially, she was able to return to the family briefly, which helped her further heal a little, too. By now she had accepted both herself and him. She had given up her illusions, replacing them with a certain gratitude that her struggle with him had contributed significantly to who she was as a person.

In the process of "facing the lion," in other words, we have altered both our needs and our perceptions because we now stand firmly in touch with our loving center. External situations don't necessarily change, but the way we hold them or see them *does* change. We move now from a different base. This knowledge of self, this confidence in that strengthened core, is the "pearl beyond price" about which the mystics and saints have written. We should congratulate ourselves for the journey, for it has most likely been a hard-won victory.

6

Peace
at Last:

New Directions Emerge

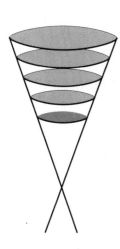

Emily's parents were shocked and saddened at her decision to leave Kansas City for a job as co-director of a medical clinic in California. Why would she leave her secure technician position? Somehow they had expected their eldest daughter to live near them forever.

Emily had known for some time, however, that her life in the Midwest was over. The wounds from digging up a painful childhood felt healed, and she enjoyed sound friendships with her four children. All were successfully launched, or nearly so, into lives of their own. Having worked hard to resolve her turmoil the past few years, she wasn't too sure herself what moving West meant. But she knew she was responding to an inner call and a new-found ability to risk. She felt drawn to the ocean and a professional environment that would expand her skills. The clinic would mean a career shift from individual work to growth as a manager. In fact, when it came right down to it, she knew she had little choice in the matter. Emily had to pursue this opening now, before she lost her nerve.

The feeling that one must follow "thy will, not mine" is a common turning point as we emerge from the depths of the growth process. Emily reached this conclusion after considerable reflection; others may discover it more abruptly. One CEO, who faced a Chapter 11 bankruptcy reorganization before he realized that money was not the God, found this willingness at the end of a day when everything had again gone wrong. Sales had been off for months, but this was the second month in a row he'd been unable to make payroll. As he drove blindly down the freeway, tears rolled down his cheeks;

he sent up a silent prayer for help. Suddenly he realized the turning point available. He had missed all the signs because his ego had been so damaged by this "failure."

In a flash the CEO saw it differently. Bankruptcy reorganization was perfectly acceptable; he could create a better company in the process, and someday he would share his story with others. That, of course, was what he was supposed to do, not be a millionaire as he once thought. The quality of the relationships among his employees and whether they felt part of the team now mattered more than other things. Of course they had to be profitable, but *how* they did that was most important. In fact, maybe treating people differently was the missing clue. His mind turned to how he could create a role for a president; his vice-president, the logical choice, was a better delegator than he was. If he turned more day-to-day management over to him and focused on creative aspects himself, things might run much better. Everyone probably needed more authority, especially the vice-president, he mused. If he could just get out of the way and let them do their jobs. The vice-president could give him frequent reports so he wouldn't feel out of touch. The CEO knew he would have to work hard at not meddling, but he realized that what was required now was to "follow" rather than try so hard to control the outcome.

At this stage in the process, one begins to rest more in a state of inner peace and happiness. Intuition and creativity begin to flow. Loneliness is a thing of the past because we have found a core "self;" we experience companionship with ourselves. New decisions about life directions are apt to be made, usually in response to vague but compelling urges that come from beyond our selfish interests. Obeying this deeper will implies an acceptance that powers greater than oneself exist; we are more likely to believe that universal wisdom/harmony can be tapped it we will follow these inner signals.

IDENTIFYING CHARACTERISTICS
1. Inner peace, blissful moments, mystical knowing

Ruth's description of a blissful 10-day period in 1986 sums up one of the best indications that healing was finally taking root. "The days slipped by with a serenity and happiness that seemed impossible before—as though I was gliding on a calm sea that was totally without inner turmoil. Customers responded to my calls as if I had magic. Co-workers felt like family for the first time. The quiet joy of this interlude was so extraordinary that I felt slightly fearful." Ruth's uneasiness came from the fact that we become so wedded to struggle as a way of life that we are disturbed by its absence. During Being/Resolution/Acceptance we experience longer and longer periods of genuine inner peace. Our lives take on added fullness as we sense growing confidence that the worst has been weathered.

Ruth's new state of mind was based upon having come to terms with her past, plus a growing clarity about her future. Having climbed the ladder to a mid-level financial management position in several corporations, she now knew she wanted to be in business for herself. She wanted to create a company with flexible options and more humane values. Several other women and a few semi-retirees in her church group had all expressed the desire for jobs that could be done on a 20-30 hour basis. Some also wanted generous "time outs" for travel or children's vacations. Ruth thought she knew how to build in flexibility from the beginning; the right mix of employees would need to cover for each other, but she thought she could develop that teamwork. Deciding whether to buy an existing business or create a new one was the major question. That would take some time to investigate; augmenting her savings to cover her son's education was another immediate need. She began to develop a three year transition plan.

2. Creativity from one's center

Bernie's first indication that he might be far more creative than he had imagined came rather suddenly. Over a period of several weeks, the idea for producing a training video on multi-media presentations took shape. During his many management presentations, his audiences had asked as often about the audio-visual techniques as about the speech content. Now might be the time to pull some "how-to's" together. As the ideas flowed out, he was amazed at the inspiration. A certain deadness and pain had been so dominant for months that he almost took it for granted. But now he was feeling recharged; in fact, he was somewhat awed with the breakthrough. Ideas had never flowed so quickly, so cohesively before.

As Bernie reflected that maybe his inner struggle might be lifting, he became excited about the possibilities for bringing out creativity in other people. He knew there was a connection between the emotional work he'd been doing and this recent surge. In an instant he saw that probably everyone had untapped creativity within them; the books he'd read on innovation, however, didn't describe this relationship between inner growth and creative capacity. He was convinced that such self-development was an overlooked key.

Bernie's thoughts jumped from the video to musings about his staff. What would happen, he wondered, if he shared his personal breakthroughs with them? Might they be inspired to seek similar growth? Would they need an external crisis, such as his divorce had been, to awaken them? Was pain always necessary to produce change? Was he really ready to tell them about his own therapy and how it had made such a difference? So much had changed for him in recent years, including how he viewed himself as a father and a man. He felt like he'd been peeling off excess layers for months. Now the boss role was shifting too. Bernie wasn't yet sure how to strike the balance between being overly personal and wanting to serve as model, but he decided to begin with several staff people. There were a few employees who particularly seemed ready to consider the subject of inner growth.

The contrast between the creativity Bernie was feeling now and his former years was striking. Always before he had been considered a competent, hard working manager, but he had striven laboriously for those results. "Creative" would not have been a word that described him. Persistence and dedicated were more appropriate. Now, however, he could see that his previous lack of creativity was due mainly to psychological blocks, inner doubts and negative self-beliefs. Removing the negatives had freed untapped energy; he found a capacity to make new connections. He was as eager to share these insights as he was the video.

Describing how this creativity worked, however, might be difficult, for there was something different about the breakthrough. Now it felt as though the ideas came from his center rather than his head. Writing those earlier speeches had been full of painstaking effort. This time, however, the video ideas emerged from somewhere deep inside. Shaping them would still take effort, but there was something indescribably different. Experiencing the difference made him feel as though he had become a participant or a receiver in the creative process. His whole being was somehow involved.

3. Self-love, trust in self, freedom from worry

Bill felt surprisingly relaxed about shifting his career to adult education consulting. Leaving the state bureaucracy would be a relief. As head of the investigations unit, the hours, tight budgets and staff turnover had become steadily worse. He had tried to carry too much of the burden himself. Over the last several years, however, since the stroke, he had changed his diet, his daily living habits and many of his outlooks. Living a balanced life had become a major goal. To achieve it, he and his wife, Marilyn, had pursued long hours of counseling. He carefully saved quality time for the children, and he made sure that he and Marilyn went away for a weekend every several months. Genuine fun and intimacy prevailed in the family; Bill was at peace with himself these days.

Bill now understood why he'd been a driven workaholic before the stroke. Professional commitment had been part of it; he had strong feelings about excellence and serving the public. The major reason, however, for practically killing himself, had been the holdover effect of trying to please a father for whom even Herculean efforts were never enough. Proving himself had gone on and on even after his father's death. Now that past could no longer haunt him. Major questions loomed about how to make a career shift and support the family, but he knew if he pursued his inner direction that doors would open. His wife was eager to lend her emotional and financial support.

The ability to trust in ourselves, believing that we will be guided toward solutions, is a hallmark of this stage. Past, present and future blend together in a state of contentment as we consider new options. Sometimes we wonder if we're being "irresponsible" to be so trusting; at other times this sense of being anchored in a new level of reality, a very different self, is hard to describe. In a psychological sense we have begun to tap into our core center where the capacity to love ourselves and others resides (Lowen, 1975, p. 120). Beneath the layers of psychic defenses that have been penetrated lies a sense of self that is beyond everyday problems or worries. This does not mean that problems evaporate; instead, you notice them without them dominating your existence (Wilber, 1979, pp. 128-130).

Part of the reason why this state is so difficult to talk about is that it is a part of self that is beyond words. We have forged this central part of our being by clearing many defense layers, conflicts and boundaries that felt extremely emotional. The sense of quiet, depth and knowingness that emerges seems almost to be without distinguishing qualities. We bask for a while in feeling somehow above it all, or free at last from negative emotions.

4. Healing the man within; mourning loss

Linda Leonard writes extensively about "healing the man within" in *The Wounded Woman: Healing the Father/Daughter Relationship.* Her book is about more than her personal experience; it is also about healing patriarchal wounds. To heal the inner man means to find the positive, masculine side of self that is caring and warm, able to love, playful and productive, sensual and creative. This "man" knows limits and boundaries but also possesses a soaring spirit that takes us beyond ourselves. In our patriarchal culture, "the man within" has often been severely disrupted from being a healthy, positive image for both women and men. Whether the male energy takes the form of the perverted, authoritarian father or the rebellious little boy, the patriarchy in general has not encouraged human wholeness. Both individual lives and our work environments have correspondingly suffered.

Healing the wound might be a slightly different experience for women and men. A woman, for example may be more aware of the masculine energy through the figures in her dream life. As men's gatherings show us, however, a good many men also need to heal this inner-outer figure. The fact that our psychological development has been frozen at the adolescent stage, on incomplete male images, has profound implications for both sexes.

My inner man became healed as I came to terms with my father's terminal illness. The inner figures were reflected in dream characters, such as the rebellious little boy who wet his pants or who asked for help. Over a period of several months, as it became clear that my father was dying, the grieving and healing process unfolded. It was summed up in a letter I wrote to thank him for the contributions to my life. These included strong independence training, a model for being in business and his financial preparations. The latter had freed me over the years to pursue my own dreams. Only lately had I become conscious that identifying with him meant that my life, like so many other career women, had been much more male-adapted than female until now. Thus, this inner journey had been a profound recovery of the feminine.

Behind the letter, however, lay my internal process of forgiving him for what he had *not* done. The lack was summed up in one of our conversations about his dying. When I asked whether or not he was afraid to die, the answer was a firm "no." He said he had done what he wanted to with his life, namely build a successful business. Not a word was mentioned about being a good husband or a good father. The omission stung me; his words reflected our failed relationship. Quite simply, he had never been available emotionally because he had not been present for himself. Yet ironically, our closed doors as father/daughter had opened my heart. His rejection, both past and present, had so often been the trigger to push me deeper into growth. As I reviewed our years together yet so far apart, I could see both grandeur and despair woven in every step. The man so responsible for much of my wounding was the same person who had provided the fighting spirit to go beyond it.

As his illness grew worse, I was comforted by a series of dreams with positive masculine figures. One of the most poignant was about a man who needed to cry as much as I had cried, and that I could comfort him. Such comforting had actually happened through my letter, but "the man" can also be understood as the masculine consciousness of our time. All of us need to be healed of the wounds of the patriarchy, to find the man within who is both supportive and inspiring.

In my case my father represented both the wounder and the wounded. His masculine side was over-developed, just like our present culture; his feminine side was deficient. He had been a classic example of the authoritarian patriarch who worked hard, made decisions alone and insisted on being right. Work was his primary focus. The long hours were justified as doing it "for the family," but I could see now that flight from intimacy had also driven him away. The result was an incomplete person. Staying trapped in that masculine role meant that he never moved beyond ego consciousness, despite his feeling for music and a talent for wisdom and laughter. Sadly, he had not had the opportunity to develop a balanced relationship with himself, much less with others, except in a limited way. The tragedy was that he would never do his crying.

My sorrow went very deep. I shed tears about his wasted potential and the fact that our relationship had been a failed one. The loss could only be mourned. Each time I wept I felt lighter. As the inner healing occurred, some relationships with male colleagues softened and felt more balanced. I could be myself with them now without strain. Certain client relationships, however, proved more difficult. The better I felt about me, the less desire I had to work with those who remained unconscious. The roles they were playing appeared unreal, unauthentic. Their insensitivity to one another felt abrasive and harmful.

5. Synchronicity, grace, external support

Carl Jung and others who have investigated the phenomenon of synchronicity suggest that such events often accompany breakthroughs in personal growth. Certainly this stage represents one of those thresholds; if an intense emotional experience accompanies this passage, the synchronicity can be prolonged.

Janice couldn't believe how her co-workers responded when it became known that her husband had been abusive before she finally walked out. The corporate legal counsel and his wife insisted she stay with them until she could find her own place. Two division managers helped her prioritize the mid-winter conference to relieve her of all but the tasks that only she could do. People from the rest of the organization that she hadn't seen in months called for lunch, a drink or came by for a desk-side chat. It was a week or more of incredible grace, of having genuine needs met by a supportive world.

Despite Janice's outward crisis, the days flowed smoothly, from one thing to the next, in a sort of timeless rhythm and peace. She asked her boss if he had noticed these small events, but he had not. Yes, he thought she was coping well, but he had not noticed much unusual. Thus, although synchronicity appears to operate most frequently during important transitions, such as death, birth or falling in love, the awareness that it was present had much to do with her inner state. Janice had grown significantly in recent years. Not only was she strong enough to refuse to be abused; she also had the capacity at this point to appreciate that the phone rang at the right moment or that someone offered exactly the right words. She felt enormously comforted amidst her upheaval.

Overall, this quality called "grace" is a sense of profound gratitude for the gift of life. During such moments we pause to appreciate both large and small things, the pain as well as the joy. It is a feeling that things really do make sense and have purpose after all. Even the death of a loved one or the onset of an emotional crisis has a beauty and a "rightness" to it if we are emotionally clear enough to allow the feelings to flow through without becoming stuck in fear or grief.

6. Endings, detachments, reflective loss

During this stage of our passage, there is a sense of needing to complete things, to say goodbye and to mourn their loss or passing in a quiet way. Tears may flow and problems may be present, but much of the pain beneath this passage has already been expelled. The sense of death or loss that surrounds this time has a softer, more reflective tone than the grief of the previous stage. Sadly, we become aware that we have grown beyond certain people, jobs, or geographical locations. The detachment process has already been initiated, and there is an urgency now about moving on to new activities.

Marie, for example, was aware that she had done what she could as a training director in a small corporation. Over the past two years she had created 10 new skills workshops on everything from project management to conflict resolution and creativity. She knew the sessions had brought the supervisors to a new level of sophistication. Being able to reinforce the learning with follow-up coaching had been especially rewarding. The company was so tightly knit that she could see and feel the culture change. Meetings now were shorter and highly task-oriented but often filled with laughter. People seldom complained anymore; there was a new spirit of teamwork and pride. The crazy practice of writing lots of memos in such a small place had been replaced by frequent one-on-one meetings or small group sessions.

Marie relished the thought that her efforts had made a difference to the company; she took the opportunity to have lunch with each supervisor before hiring her own replacement. Her personal life was also changing; the last daughter was now in college and would soon be job-hunting too. Marie found her own new job as director of a nonprofit organization before she initiated the resignation process. She saved time, however, to mark the endings in her life with a transition period of visits with her children and lessened social activity. Within several years she planned to move to another city; in the meantime, she surveyed her home and furnishings, mentally beginning the process of paring down the load of material possessions.

7. Following "thy will, not mine"

As with Emily who moved cross-country and the CEO who found new meaning in bankruptcy, the prompting to follow inner urges is characteristic of this stage. Some people leap off into new ventures without much fore-thought; others seem literally propelled into major changes, while still others undertake it with some planning. Often the impetus to take the next step comes in the form of faint inner signals beneath the din of daily life. How acutely we listen to these voices, as well as how much freedom we feel to follow their unknown outcome, may be a fateful decision. If we decide we must obey these promptings, frequently others in our lives will react with surprise or even resistance. To follow one's own destiny requires courage; often its pursuit doesn't make clear, rational sense, and some people may be threatened by major changes or by losing us. Those who are security-bound or who have not explored their own growth will be unable to grasp the meaning or the reasons for our restlessness.

Don and Susan, for example, heard the call to move to the Southwest where he could pursue his art while she would switch from Girl Scout executive to law school student. Scout work had awakened her interest in environmental law. Don's decision to take early retirement from the phone company would mean a small base income. Selling the house would buy at least 18 months of school for Susan. How much longer they could survive beyond that wasn't certain, but they both knew that corporate life had become a rat race. As they prepared to leave the East, they calculated how long they could live without any income; they also concluded that working at menial jobs for a while would be acceptable until they could solidify a new niche. Few of their friends could comprehend why they would give up good jobs and a lovely suburban home to pursue such a "wild goose chase." Don and Susan, however, had long since passed the point of needing or wanting their home.

Moving to a smaller apartment sounded inviting, and they were eager to shift gears.

8. Surfacing residues of grief

Patty had already quit her job with a Minneapolis computer company. For several months afterwards she read all the books she never had time for when she worked so hard as a programmer. She also wrote poetry and practiced her flute. When she visited her friend, Gordon, in Massachusetts, she learned that he and several others were starting a computer and personnel business. The trip had been planned purely as a social visit, but she knew immediately that she wanted to be part of this start-up. Patty was ready to join an entrepreneurial team.

Upon return to Minneapolis, Patty put her house up for sale. The months that followed were draining ones, as she dealt with various endings. Several cousins, who were close to her, were involved in unhappy marriages. Her father was still drinking, and her brother was on drugs. All of them had depended upon her to keep the peace. Now, however, Patty was moving on. She had known for some time that this day was coming, but family relation-ships still dangled.

Surprisingly, her father supported her move, but the others resisted. The period until her house sold in the fall was one of confronting unpleasant scenes, including a failed attempt at getting her brother to seek treatment; cutting the emotional ties with these people was difficult. Patty found it helpful to actively grieve her losses by writing, taking long walks and performing some solitary rituals that helped her let go. Mostly she was sorry her family chose not to make the changes that might make their lives happier. Yes, they were still her family, but she would be relating to them now from both a geographical and an emotional distance; their choices could no longer be hers. By the time she finally made the move East, she needed several months to rest. Dealing with all of them had taken an emotional toll. Fortunately, the start-up didn't need her immediately.

While the earlier stages of growth often focus on grieving the losses that stem from childhood, at this stage there may be surprising residues of a slightly different form of grief. These are the traumatic episodes we've encountered as adults.

By the time I attended a Kubler-Ross workshop on "Life, Death and Transition," for example, I had completed most of my childhood grieving and that for my father. The five day experience, however, was a time to cry along with some others who had also lost a parent. This was a modest emotional cleansing compared to the unexpected discovery of unresolved grief from having been a Vietnam-era veteran.

From 1965-69 I had been an Air Force Intelligence officer, primarily briefing flight crews and general staff. This meant being stationed with the B-52 bombing operations on Guam and Okinawa. Being involved in the war effort had troubled me, but I had long since buried such thoughts. Now, some 20 years later, I was awash with sadness as both Vietnam veterans and war protestors shared their stories in the workshop.

I had no idea such intense emotions about Vietnam were lying dormant. They emerged full force from several of us, including an executive, an unemployed vet, a controller, a retired Major, several draft resistors, a therapist and me. Whether the stories came from combat soldiers or deserters, it was clear that all of us had been caught in an immense tragedy. Anger, guilt, confusion, helplessness and terror came tumbling out. One of the most surprising facets of this purging was that it didn't matter what side we had been on or what our actions had been, whether to serve the country or to leave it; what was apparent was that all of us had been ripped apart by Vietnam. Some of the stories told by those who saw ground combat were horrendous. My stomach turned upside down several times; tears of empathy and sorrow poured down my cheeks as I heard their anguish. Certainly my participation as a briefing officer had been nothing by comparison, yet the emotional impact had been deep.

After the Vietnam stories had been shared, the larger group staged a healing ritual for us. They "welcomed us home" symbolically, something the country had never done. The half dozen of us receiving this belated tribute remembered the scorn we'd received as returning veterans. Now we stood linked arm-in-arm, crying like babies for an hour. That "ceremony" remains one of the most memorable episodes in my healing process; it was an example of what needs to happen nationally to help heal our festering wounds.

The mark of a healing experience is that it gives us emotional release from something painful in the past. Such healing can be facilitated by an individual, but it is far more powerful when coming from a group. Usually we feel cleansed, refreshed and relieved afterwards, as though the weight of years has been lifted. Such healing usually requires the presence of unconditional love in some form, including the ability to hear someone out without judgment. The willingness to be fully present in an emotional sense as someone reexperiences their pain can be enormously helpful. When such an attitude of compassionate understanding comes from a group, the effect is powerful beyond words.

9. Being tested; finding inner support and balance

Actually there are many tests of courage, skill and readiness along the path of inner growth, yet there comes a time when an outward event or several looms large as a test of just how far we've come. Being/Resolution/Acceptance is often that point, as though this is a summing up before we continue.

Todd's test came when he received notice that he had not survived the latest management reduction. For years he had done his best to support each boss who was presented after the company's frequent reorganizations. Now he had nothing to lose by speaking out. He went to the vice-president with whom he had worked on several task forces to have his final say. First he quietly admitted his anger. Then he pointed out how the abrupt changes in direction had hampered his department. Better teamwork could have prevented or alleviated much of the disruption, but communicating with "the old man" was generally considered a lost cause. Thus, he and his counterparts had been forced to play continual survival games. Todd now wished in hindsight that he had been stronger about resisting; not going along, however, would have been suicide under the circumstances. The vice-president tried to interrupt Todd several times with explanations or rebuttal. Todd, however, quickly asserted that excuses were no longer sufficient. He'd heard enough defensiveness in this organization to last a lifetime. At this point he had few hopes that his remarks would make a difference, but he was determined to speak the truth. Todd needed the best of his "tough love" skills to make his points. The corporation had used him unfairly, he said. Only too late had he seen that he too was responsible; standing up to be counted earlier might have made the difference, but much of the situation was beyond his control. This reduction was merely the cumulative effect of many previous bad decisions.

Todd pointed out that other lives were needlessly being uprooted far more than his would be. He suggested that the fault should be shared by those above, who, unfortunately, appeared unwilling to accept any responsibility. Todd was neither bitter nor belligerent, but he was very firm. The vice-president listened quietly for 10 more minutes. He seemed uneasy as he walked Todd to the door. Todd felt good about the exchange; he had used his new-found clarity to put things straight.

At this stage in our growth we understand how to support ourselves and how to walk away with dignity. Sometimes a similar strength can be used to change the situation without the need to end it.

10. Intuition becomes reliable; sense of flow is natural

Throughout the stories in this chapter runs a similar thread of people finding more and more trust in themselves and their *inner* reaction to external events. Patty, for example, trusted her intuition to get her through the words and deeds involved in family endings. Todd trusted his instincts in dealing with the vice-president in new ways, while Don and Susan and Emily all trusted the signals they were getting about career changes.

Because intuition is such a critical faculty, however, it bears mention as a separate characteristic. The ability to employ it, to listen to the "still small voice within," grows ever-stronger with practice. Yet at this level, we really start to *act* upon this information. We are likely at this point to put intuition in charge rather than allowing rational thinking to dominate. What is now possible is a shift in our emphasis, or a change in priority about the way we work with these capacities. As our core self becomes stronger, rational thinking is used as support to the intuitive. Thus, we get the inner hunch about a decision or a direction to pursue, then we back it up by checking out the facts or analyzing the situation. A chain store owner, for example, gets a hunch about the timing and location for a new store. He goes to the general area to see how it feels and looks, smiling when he arrives because it does seem right. There are several vacant buildings that seem possible; one in particular draws his attention. He starts envisioning the busy operations here. Before deciding, however, he compares land values and consults traffic analysis and growth pattern reports. Finally, he returns to the proposed location several times to see if the feelings and facts are in sync.

The reason that intuition becomes more reliable is that we have reached a place where we can tap more easily into our central core. To truly anchor this self that is beyond ego requires much more practice, yet here is where we begin to trust inner harmony and balance. The major boundaries of our defense system have been penetrated or opened so that intuitive wisdom can come through on a more constant basis. Emotional blockages have been cleared to open the channel. This core center of self, this intuitive faculty, is described in many ways, such as "listening to the inner voice," contacting the "higher self," or tuning into the intuitive, all-knowing portion of self. Religious expressions of it are "the inner light," the divinity in each person, the "kingdom of God within," the Godself and the immortal soul that is an all-loving, source of guidance. Whatever its name, it is the source of new internal clarity, vision and wisdom.

This new guidance mechanism can be used in both large and small ways to guide our decision-making and actions. A manager, for example, sensing that something personal was troubling an employee, used it to figure out how to deal with the woman. The issues were extremely delicate. The work flow was being disturbed, which was unusual, and morale was suffering in the claims unit. The manager took the issue home with her; on her evening walk, she quietly asked herself how she might approach this person. Then she stopped thinking about it as she completed the walk and did the evening chores. In the morning, several approaches occurred to the manager. She knew instinctively she must combine strong personal support with a message that the employee's performance was suffering. Otherwise the woman would just clam up. Approaching her on exactly the right foot would mean that the underlying problem might be solved.

Similarly, we can use intuition to address major life questions if we have done enough clearing work to hear and see the answers. Often we must quiet ourselves to get in touch, but we can ask ourselves (or our unconscious) what to do about major projects, personal relationships or career changes. Then we must be attuned to the words in a book, the conversation with another or the passing thought that sheds new light on the subject. Usually these inner signals are not "loud" answers, but if they are valid, they will persist or be amplified.

One of the most satisfying results of this switch from external to internal control is that we naturally become more adventuresome and able to take risks. To do so, however, does not mean to take foolish risks. Nonetheless, people who have come this far are relatively free of the interfering "noise" from social conditioning that blocks natural intuition. Most of us, however, still have much work to do to further integrate our physical, emotional, intellectual and spiritual components. We may feel strong enough or safe enough to make commitments to major directions about becoming more fully ourSelves, but we need more practice before inner authority reigns supreme.

COPING STRATEGIES
1. Follow inner promptings without being naive
Some people don't make the transition to new jobs, careers or geographical locations as easily as those in my examples. In fact, some don't make it at all. This is usually because they didn't have enough money to last the duration, didn't make realistic plans, weren't willing to make appropriate sacrifices or work at intermediate jobs. In other words, they had more lessons of personal mastery before they were ready to "Follow thy will, not mine." Some of them also don't completely finish their emotional "unfinished business," such as dealing with family relationships, so they are pulled back to complete this piece. Some people forever avoid the indepth clearing work required of middle stages. Their surface attention to this work thus stunts the quality and depth of renewal.

The suggestion is clear: Don't leap off into the unknown without some clear evaluation of the risks and consequences that you personally must consider. Stories about people living out of cars while they pursue new directions are not uncommon. When one becomes committed to following one's path, however, only individuals can assess how much risk is possible. Circumstances vary widely, but it is wise to consider that making a major transition usually takes longer than we think. The other side of the coin, however, is that we would probably not set out at all if we fully knew the future. Being tested about our commitment to this path is part of what growth involves. As we proceed, there will be more doubts, fears and uncertainty to conquer. Those who do successfully "Follow thy will, not mine," however, do not do it by being impetuous or without being willing to be responsible for their actions.

2. Allow reflection time, mourning, cleaning up
By January of 1988 Shana was ready to leave Denver. Burned out at work, she had resigned as branch manager of a title company. Somewhat against her better judgment, she had agreed to finish up several projects on a consulting basis while she waited for her house to sell. This proved to be a valuable time to reflect, mourn and dispose of possessions. Cleaning out

office files, books and boxes was a therapeutic process in itself; each load of books given to the library, each bag of trash and each donated item of furniture made her feel freer.

Another benefit was the opportunity to interact in new ways with the remaining management team. Initially their offer of the consulting projects had seemed a compliment. Now, however, she could see that it was more of their surface support; in the past, many project innovations in everything from performance appraisal to new filing systems had often been hers, but implementation was slow in the face of their objections; the credit she received was begrudging and slight. In many ways Shana realized she had been invisible to these men.

This time when she brought the finished reports to the team, she called them on their subtle put-downs. She refused to be interrupted; she presented her ideas forcefully, and she moderated the discussion with purposeful direction. She let them know that stalling tactics would be costly in time and dollars. In fact, her time was extremely limited these days. When she was criticized, she didn't take it personally. Shana could feel a strengthened center of self. Her command of herself sometimes felt shaky, but her voice was convincing and calm. Beyond these clean-up projects, she saw that she could do little more in this organization. She wasn't being valued to the extent that she had learned to value herself. It was time to move on to a place and circumstances where bravado was unnecessary. The armor had been needed to survive in an unsupportive environment. Shana's departing confrontation about the dynamics she saw operating represented a minor victory. Behind it was her conviction that male authority, control and approval no longer mattered. To be free enough to walk away from the need for this approval is something that many more women need to experience if we are to become free of the patriarchy.

Shana's additional benefit from this period was simply the time to reflect quietly and to say some proper goodbyes. This was a happy kind of mourning. Memories of the solace that this home had provided flooded through her; events of the past 20 years were reviewed with relish; she carefully planned each farewell with a friend. Always before such rites of passage had been neglected; she had rushed into the next change before the old had been completed. This time she did the leave-taking properly.

3. Enhance or explore your budding creativity

During the last several years, the business world has discovered that creativity and intuition are important to develop. Furthermore, many consultants believe that such skills can be taught or enhanced. The number of workshops and books on creativity, intuition and innovation has leaped dramatically. You might be able to capitalize on your creative talent by attending a seminar or doing further reading. So far, however, there is little understanding among trainers that true creativity springs from within and is dependent upon clearing emotional blocks. Nonetheless, training can be a worthwhile exploration. Understanding your personal right/left brain style, for example, can be useful; participating in a seminar where styles and techniques are presented can be fun and helpful.

In the future, creativity training will probably be standard for all workers and children, but right now it is still one of our recent "discoveries." The good news, however, is that enhanced creativity is a natural by-product of inner growth. Creativity, in other words, is widespread in the population, as the management theorist, Douglas McGregor, long ago pointed out. When we understand the part that maturation plays in unblocking this resource, then businesses may become very interested in psychological growth.

4. Celebrate yourself!

Most of us are very poor at celebration and rewards. The desire for play and celebration, however, becomes stronger as one moves through the stages. Now is a good time to celebrate yourself with a vacation, a special purchase, a deserved rest, occasions with friends or something that creates the feeling of congratulation. No, the work is not yet done, but this stage is a definite watershed. Arriving here does not mean that we are finished with growth. Indeed, it seems as though the journey never ends. Nonetheless, reaching this point constitutes the major healing portion of the spiral. That realization deserves to be noticed and acclaimed.

7

Unpacking
the Core:
Surprising Episodes

For three weeks the energy waves, out-of-body dreams, relentless insights and mystical experiences poured in without relief. Life was infused with meaning; every event, from TV news to phone calls, seemed loaded with symbolism. My journal from this period is inches thick; writing in it was the only way to "empty" myself to be ready for further input. Oceanic waves of consciousness rolled over me, waking me at odd hours and keeping me awake for many more with restless bursts of ideas.

At times I was frightened; often I was elated and awed. Rereading the journal notes tells me that some of the infusion was pure imagination. Other evidence, however, indicates hours of inspiration and far-seeing wisdom. Daily living itself had also been affected. Simple tasks, such as grocery shopping or getting dressed, were complicated by preoccupation with other-worldly thoughts. I hunted often for misplaced shoes or remembered to stop at the store only blocks after passing the shopping center.

Such periods of illumination have occurred throughout history to religious figures, poets and philosophers. While still uncommon today, there is reason to believe that such states are becoming less rare. Those who undertake rigorous inner work are prime candidates.

Just how many people have gone through prolonged periods of illuminating breakthrough, or what might determine whether people do or don't pass through this barrier awaits further research. The fact is that we know far too little about the later stages of growth. They seem to involve a spiritual deepening, a consolidation of previous work and creative visioning. Other characteristics include a period of "no self," when external definitions and previous achievements cease to matter. Diet and exercise become important because we are trying to balance new energies with the physical body.

Creativity in general becomes a reliable quality during these years; other energy infusions can occur repeatedly. Each occurrence, however, is easier to handle and can bring us closer to a focused vision of our unique purpose. Along with clarification about our special contribution in life, there emerges the ability to maintain a present-centered harmony on a more constant basis.

IDENTIFYING CHARACTERISTICS
1. Period of "no self"; companionship with self

After the move from Denver, I cut my expenses in half. I also reduced living space to a one bedroom apartment. Paring down and simplifying was a relief. Driving cross-country to begin this new chapter was deeply satisfying. I was especially proud that I had regained enough confidence to relocate. After the fears and vulnerabilities of recent years, the courage to set out anew was important.

For months after arrival, I lived the life of a virtual recluse. At first I slept a lot and had little interest in socializing. I was emotionally exhausted from the previous months of probing self-discovery. As I met people at the swimming pool or church, I balked about supplying the usual background data. Information about where I was from, what I had done or what degrees I held seemed totally irrelevant. In fact, for a few weeks I could barely remember any details myself, about former relationships, places or events. It was as though my past and all that had gone into that identity had become a blank screen. None of the previous markers mattered, although later I would reclaim this personal history.

Besides feeling strangely devoid of a past, I was aware during these months that I was, at bottom, an essentially simple person. That meant being uncomplicated, without problems. My needs and wants seemed simple. Perhaps, I mused to myself, I was not even very deep. After years of feeling somehow "special" in my isolation, or of feeling misunderstood by others, the discovery that I might be a simple soul with simple needs was freeing.

During this suspended period of "no self," any vision of what lay ahead was absent, except in vague outline. Yet I felt unworried and peaceful. Daily chores were accomplished with rhythm and ease; swimming and basking in the sun were a tonic. Before this sojourn, the uncertainty about who I was or what I wanted in precise terms had been extremely uncomfortable; now I was content to drift, enjoying the days in small ways. Explaining this to other people usually proved impossible. Often I ended up telling them that I had "retired" early. That, however, usually created a false impression that I was wealthy. Generally I remained tight-lipped. People thought me mysteriously aloof during this period.

2. Diet and exercise changes; balancing new energies

Jim and Peggy had long been interested in gourmet cooking. As they progressed through midlife, however, they found rich sauces, red meat and dairy products offensive. Their digestive tracts reacted to this heavy fare, even though neither had medical problems or high cholesterol. More and more they turned to recipes that called for fruit juice sweeteners, ground turkey and egg whites. Eventually they gathered enough material for a cookbook for their friends.

Jim and Peggy were exhibiting a common reaction to the later stages of growth; the high fat, sugar-filled food in the American diet becomes noticeably uncomfortable; the body itself seems to know that it needs refinement in order to function at higher levels. Choices to avoid alcohol, exercise regularly and become more vegetarian are made more easily because we are listening now to a set of inner messages. Our system has been going through a purifying process; in these later stages the new psychic energies must be balanced with the physical. A pure progression toward these refinements, however, is not usually the case. We move in-and-out, up-and-down, over several years as we chip away at stubborn habits.

3. Energy surges; illumination; cosmic consciousness

During 1986 I was introduced to the first of a three week process that was to be repeated four more times over succeeding years. During the initial episode, I was inundated with energies, strange emotions and internal experiences that were hard to handle. Among my symptoms were out-of-body dreams, proceeded by a whirling sensation, as though I was being whisked away into space where I then looked down at myself in bed. Information about Goddess figures flowed into my head one afternoon, as did insights about the structure of the psyche, dream patterns, the nature of relationships and reincarnation. Several of these psychologically oriented subjects had long been of interest to me; I moved to my bookshelf to consult all the Jung volumes when the information about the psyche appeared. The input seemed an expansion of Jung's ideas.

To deal with the infusion, I made voluminous journal notes. Sometimes these felt like profound insights; other notations now look like flights of fancy. They were the result of hours spent playing with thoughts, patterns, numbers and conjectures. Part of the fascination was the discovery that I had been recording a large number of precognitive dreams during previous months.

Fortunately, I had few everyday responsibilities during this onslaught; I was still in transition from consulting to writing. Managing a job or a family would have made things difficult. The energy surges woke me at strange hours, leaving me periodically exhausted yet exhilarated. What was going on? When would it stop? Overall, I slept only three to five hours each night. Besides being bombarded with incoming material, life was infused with great meaning, as though I could understand everything. Further healing of some old emotional wounds occurred; my body felt like it was being physically realigned one afternoon. Feelings of awe, love, gratitude and reverent appreciation filled me. Nonetheless, the experience disrupted daily living; it felt so bizarre that I kept it to myself, wishing that things would calm down to their former serene pace. Gradually, during the fourth week, they did.

Not until several years later did I discover that several thousand others had also been visited by similar episodes. Most have been helped by the Spiritual Emergence Network (SEN) that made on-call professional people available to persons in the midst of such an explosion. Such episodes can be terrifying, even dangerous.

Many instances of similar awakenings in poets, philosophers and religious figures were identified by Richard Bucke in 1900 in the now-classic *Cosmic Consciousness*. According to Bucke, the prime characteristics of this awakening include "1) a consciousness of the cosmos, or of the life and order of the universe, 2) intellectual enlightenment or illumination, 3) a state of moral exaltation, elevation or elation, and 4) a sense that we all have eternal life" (Bucke, 1969, pp. 72-79). Bucke thought that illumination usually occurred in the spring or early summer, and that those who experienced it were generally in their 30s or 40s. His conjecture was that there would be an exponential growth in such happenings until eventually it would become a birthright.

A more contemporary explanation about these vast energies is that they constitute the famed "serpent power" of Kundalini, known for years by Eastern yogis. According to Niccola Kester in an article on Kundalini, the SEN recorded an increase in Westerners experiencing the sometimes bizarre events that accompany Kundalini rising. Their symptoms include sensations of heat or electricity in the body, uncontrolled bodily movements, unusual breathing patterns and vocalizations, intense laughing or crying, singing, talking in tongues and making animal noises. Prolonged sleeplessness, inexplicable pain, amplified emotional reactions, confusion, loss of space or time sense, a racing mind full of insights, hearing beautiful sounds and seeing things are all manifestations.

Kester goes on to say that according to the Hindus, such surges are the creative, feminine energy of the universe. Generally it was believed that this energy could by aroused only by those with a certain physical and spiritual purity. Some, however, also thought that it could be aroused prematurely (resulting in insanity and death) or that it could be channeled in wrong ways through the body (Kester, 1989, pp. 3, 18, 20).

One man who experienced the premature Kundalini phenomenon in conjunction with a severe illness, spent the following six months on an emotional high. He also thought he had received direction during the energy onslaught to start a new company. Bankruptcy followed within several years, and he later realized that he was totally ungrounded when the vision had appeared. Many more years of work were required before he was ready to realize some of the promise from the original visions.

Just the fact that Kundalini episodes are now occurring outside the Eastern cultural context means that many people may be disoriented, frightened and angry when it happens. Frequently traditional psychiatry has responded to anyone with these symptoms with hospitalization or medication. We have called them "crazy." Instead, such persons may be among the most enlightened. We desperately need better understanding of these phenomena and how to help people through such periods.

4. Instincts erupt

Another puzzling characteristic that seemed to happen both before and after the eruptions was that my instincts emerged with astounding force. Sexuality was one of those instincts. After several years of near total celibacy, I was shocked one evening to discover my body registering waves of sexual urges *after* a man had departed from a nonsexual, friendly visit. So strong was the reaction, which lingered for days, that I thought momentarily that the desert air had swept me off my feet with some unknown elixir. When I recognized the true cause, I laughed uproariously. Later, however, I read Chris Griscom's account of orgasmic explosions she experienced alone. She labeled them "cosmic orgasms" (Griscom, 1987, pp. 95-96). Bradgon's important book, *The Call to Spiritual Emergence,* also describes the sexual component of spiritual emergence. There were other urges during the energy surge itself that seemed related to instinctual needs. They included sugar and salt cravings that made me wonder whether I was moving back into old addictive behaviors. My body needed more sugar while I was in this heightened state. My solution was not the wisest; I drank a lot of wine and even some Scotch that I hadn't touched in years. The alcohol was partly to satisfy the sugar craving and partly to hold myself down from the feeling that I would sail right off into space without an anchor. As I did so, I wondered about alcoholics who couldn't stay dry. Was there any correlation between these periods and their relapses? Something very different apparently happens with the body metabolism during the Kundalini infusions. Understanding such wild physical swings will be an important research subject in order to help others with their self-regulation as more people encounter cosmic awakenings.

Another instinct that may emerge is aggression. For me, this did not include physical aggression, but my mood was sometimes one of absolute certainty; my manner became brusque, impatient or dictatorial. I thought I knew exactly what I wanted, and I had little tolerance for slow responses from others. Such reactions sometimes frightened others; they were so unlike the person they knew.

5. Reclaiming our will; masculine/feminine balance swings

Peter Caddy, co-founder of Findhorn, a spiritual community in Scotland that was formed over 20 years ago, talks about his departure from that community in the '80s as a time when he needed to get in touch with his feminine side. Caddy had been a hard-driving, somewhat authoritarian leader. Apparently he received a strong message that he needed to become balanced. Thus, he made an abrupt switch from Findhorn to lying on the beaches of Hawaii, living a totally unstructured life for a while. This was his means of tapping the *being* side of his nature. Later, Caddy stated that he needed an adjustment period after awakening the feminine in order to reclaim his will. He had become so accustomed to nonaction and passive acceptance that he found decisive movement momentarily awkward.

Similarly, my transition from consultant to author was interrupted by the feeling that I swung ungraciously between the masculine/feminine on a daily or weekly basis. Situations that required assertive action felt cumbersome, as though I needed to learn all over again how to be tough when necessary. At other times I had little interest in exerting my will. The prolonged days of becoming feminized and softened seemed over, yet finding a new center of balance took time and practice. Both yoga and massage therapy helped me move toward equilibrium.

6. Finding feminine spirit; creativity takes hold

Jungian Linda Leonard *(The Wounded Woman)* writes about how she searched for definitions of feminine spirit after her long healing process. To heal "the man within" is not enough; we must also name and claim true feminine strength and wisdom.

To rename or understand the feminine in new ways is part of an integration process that society in general needs. Indeed, how can we validate the feminine unless we define and celebrate its presence? Until today the feminine has stood for something weaker, less than human. Such "naming" has warped self-definitions for both sexes. It has decimated some women and severely wounded the species.

Much of what I finally concluded to be essentially, proudly feminine is the inner journey itself. This means that true feminine energy can only be understood in terms of what happens during the deep personal change of psychological maturation. Thus, the best of the feminine includes making the unconscious conscious, discovering our allowing, receiving sides and becoming comfortable with *being* versus doing. Most importantly, however, feminine spirit is the unconditional love or healing power that resides within us all. We tap into that source repeatedly as we move through deep personal change. Such love and healing is the very heart of our ability to regenerate or to create.

Too often the masculine principle has been thought of as the creative force, yet that is only part of the story. Often it is the masculine that inspires us, then provides the will to bring creation into form. Creative generation, however, doesn't happen without the receptive feminine container; and the deeper the feminine side within us, the more that our inherent creativity can bloom. That container gets carved out only as we pursue inner growth. The more thoroughly that we do our emotional work, the more creative we can be.

There is still another aspect of the feminine that needs redress. This is the notion, perhaps hard to imagine, that the feminine needs to come first, not second. We need to listen first to our inward signals, then back that up with masculine action and thought. Most often we do things the opposite way— thought or action first.

The "feminine first" principle is best illustrated with a modern day story. When Sarah Ferguson, the liberated young English woman was being courted by Prince Andrew, she was asked whether she would have any trouble with saying the traditional wedding vows. Her ready quip was that she would have no problem "obeying" Andrew as long as he agreed *first* to "honor" her.

Fergie's answer was an important one; within the wedding vows, which are said between a woman and a man, is also the nugget of the right *internal* relationship between feminine and masculine. In other words, the vows suggest that we *first* honor the woman, then secondarily obey the man. Similarly, during the inner journey we learn to listen first to feminine intuition, feeling or instinct; masculine analysis, thought or action follows in support. Likewise, the development of the *relationship* between persons in a business transaction should come first, then the project itself can be undertaken. The patriarchy has confused the natural order.

7. Search for community; willingness to rejoin life

Our pursuit of inner growth can appear at times to be narcissistic self-indulgence. Indeed, it can become a selfish, preoccupation if we abandon normal responsibilities. There are stories, for example, of women walking out on husbands and children or vice-versa because the urge to follow their path was so strong. Outside of these extreme examples, however, the accusation that pursuing one's freedom is selfish is based upon total misunderstanding of the journey.

People who have done true inner homework do not usually stay inwardly focused. Although they develop autonomy and inner direction, they emerge from the process as stronger people who are ready to *serve*. Once they begin to define new directions, they search for others similarly inclined. As one woman said, "My blood family is a mess, but all of that agony is behind me. Now I want to be with other whole, healthy people who are making the world a better place to live. I'm tired of having to make it all happen myself."

Such hunger for community and interdependent living is hard to satisfy in a mobile, materialistic society. Even our houses and apartments promote isolation instead of sharing. Many religious or activist groups come together partly out of this desire for community and partly out of desire to create new environmental or social options. Many are naive about organization and many are just getting started. Nonetheless, as more and more people pursue inner growth, the net result may be increased pressures for communal sharing. Such an urge, however, does not necessarily mean communal living. The hunger for community means that once you have been through the inner process, where strong awareness of interdependence is evoked, it then appears ludicrous to live so independently.

8. "Letting go" continues; minor setbacks

Marsha thought she had finished most of her emotional clearing work; the majority had centered on her father. As she moved toward inner balance, however, she realized that letting go of her mother remained undone. While she had never identified much with mother, she knew that her parents imbalance as a couple had been the hindrance to family mental health.

Marsha's mother was a whiner and a complainer. She had worked long hours to raise the family, helping to make ends meet by doing alterations. As she plodded on, however, she let the family know she was sacrificing; she seemed to enjoy the suffering. Marsha, in turn, had received the unspoken message that she was supposed to "save" her mother from this martyrdom. Specifically, she was supposed to save the woman from perpetual loneliness and the bitter disappointments that arose from a troubled marriage.

Now Marsha began to recognize the subtle guilt trips her mother employed. In addition, nothing Marsha did for her mother ever seemed enough. The whining and complaining continued. Finally, Marsha began to withdraw from the situation. As she set limits with her mother about what she would and wouldn't do and when she would visit, the pouting scenes intensified. It was clear that Marsha was punished when she didn't kowtow to her mother's wishes. Gradually, however, the unpleasant episodes diminished. Marsha was teaching her mother that the old games no longer worked. Doing so was agonizing for Marsha, yet each time she refused to be drawn in, she felt stronger. Eventually mother and daughter reached a new arms-length understanding.

Marsha sighed with relief about completing what seemed like her last cycle of emotional baggage. The following year, however, a friend exhibited characteristics very similar to her mother's. One more time Marsha was forced to look at the dynamics in a relationship. This time she dealt with the manipulation with relative ease. The fact that she needed to do so, however, suggests that "letting go" of unfinished business continues even when we are well along the path. Such episodes, however, no longer dominate daily existence.

9. Visioning; life work or purpose clarified; fulfillment

During the ninth year of my journey, the springtime "rain of consciousness" again occurred. This time, however, the energy surge was far more focused, revealing a picture of possible future endeavors. The envisioning included the initial concept, values and structure for a business that would apply principles involved in personal and organizational transformation. The initial mission statement for this entity practically wrote itself in the early morning hours of my 44th birthday. I felt commanded to sit down and write it out.

This time I was not as frightened about the energy surges; I still lost track of time and space, but I felt more in control and less overwhelmed than I had the year earlier. Perhaps the best explanation for this change in handling the energy surges is that we become more balanced as we move along our path. The more grounded we are, the better able we are to handle this inundation from beyond the ego.

Feelings of exquisite beauty and intense meaning flooded my being even more strongly than they had before. Everything I had ever done, seen or heard seemed to have been exactly "the right thing." I could understand the significance of so much that had happened, yet I laughed at the thought that I had ever been in control of anything. It seemed as though I had been guided by unseen hands and forces from the beginning. Now I felt professionally focused as well as personally blessed beyond imagination. I knew also that the "cloud cover" overlaying life until now was gone. (Yet getting the new business off the ground would take another five years of experimentation and trial and error, not unlike the early stages of personal growth.)

Describing the majesty of the envisioning period is difficult. Afterwards I understood what the word "transcendence" means. The state where you discover this, if only in passing, is glorious, not unlike "the promised land" itself. So far our psychological literature does not give us much help in defining these states. One of the early attempts, however, came from Abraham Maslow who believed there was a stage of transcendence beyond self-actualization. Included in these qualities was the ability to lose consciousness of the ego or self and a transcendence of body, time and space. Other sensations were rising above culture, transcendence of one's past, mystic fusion, being beyond death, acceptance of the natural world, synergy, identi-fication-love, being free of the opinion of others, transcendence of dichoto-mies, embracing one's destiny, surpassing past ability and seeing wholistically easily (Maslow, 1971, pp. 269-279).

In other words, Maslow saw some differences between transcenders and merely healthy people. The transcenders valued peak experiences more, spoke the language of poets, mystics or seers, perceived the sacred in the secular yet saw practically, were motivated by higher values, were more responsive to beauty, more holistic, more synergistic, more apt to be innovators and more "religious" or "spiritual" (Maslow, 1971, pp. 283-293). There is a strong possibility that the ability to experience these peak periods is directly related to the depths of your inner work.

As more people pursue deep personal change and as societal conscious-ness shifts, there will be many more who experience the transcendent. A number of people, such as Ken Carey, who have written books such as *The Starseed Transmissions,* have obviously experienced prolonged periods of transcendence. Carey indicates that he too functioned at heights of unusual beauty and meaning.

In addition to those gifted with mystic or seeing qualities, however, there may be many who become clear about their life's purpose in less dramatic ways. As we become clear internally of the guilt, shame, anger and fear that hold us back, our unblocked guidance system functions better. We more easily move toward opportunities that can lead to personal fulfillment.

Patty, for example, thought she was paying a social visit to friends in Massachusetts. But she discovered while there that they were starting a business that was aligned with her values and special talents. In other words, once we are on track with ourselves, we attract or move toward others of similar interests, something like a radar beam honing in on its target. The number of "coincidences" in our life increases dramatically as we move forward, although their occurrence seems to be much stronger at some times than others.

10. More and more joy; happiness and contentment settle in

"I can't believe how different life looks and feels these days," said Mandy. "After all those years of moving in-and-out of depression, I see now that I don't have to exist that way anymore. Life is actually fun, and means so much more."

Mandy was 46 when she realized that things were different. It had taken two marriages, a series of other relationships and years of therapy before she knew that life could be fulfilling. In fact, her real personality, the one buried under years of conflict and confusion, emerged from the shadows. Colleagues now described her as joyful and upbeat.

The ability to experience both quiet inner joy or a noisy, outer exuberance is characteristic of later stages of growth. Rediscovering our inner child or essence means that we recapture our childlike awe and wonder. Many people report feeling blessed and rich beyond comparison, never believing that life could hold such pleasures. Buying colorful clothes, changing hair styles, developing new hobbies and having parties become reflections of this renewed zest for life. One woman realized that she had never ever experienced her childhood in the first place. She had been old far before her time. The gaiety and satisfaction she found in her middle years was thus doubly rewarding.

11. Patience, acceptance, equanimity

Those who have come through demanding inner growth have been forced to "let go" so many times that they are now able to more easily let go of positions, decisions or circumstances that appear not to be working. They recognize, sometimes almost instantly, that something should be abandoned;

furthermore, they often express faith that the next signpost will be given. Having a certain patience about life is the welcome result.

Roger's new business was a case in point. Originally he had planned to raise venture capital for an unusual production facility. As he explored the alternatives, it became clear that raising money this way required a great deal of effort and would mean losing control of the business. Quickly he abandoned this direction, opting instead for slow growth through continued market expansion. Within several years he was able to move the business from his home to an office complex; now he is developing several national markets because more and more people respect the quality of his products and service.

12. Confidence grows; flexibility; head and heart are united

Initially the new directions that emerge during renewal may seem scary. As we move through these later stages, however, we become more and more integrated and balanced. Our confidence and courage grows about next steps. The days and months dissolve in a flow that was unknown before, giving us the sense that everything is generally on track. This does not necessarily mean that all goes smoothly, but we view setbacks or problems differently. Now, even the bumps are perceived as hidden lessons for our benefit. No longer do we spend excessive time analyzing the past or agonizing about future decisions. Instead, a new inner confidence is present; despite dealing with continual uncertainty, we "know that we will know" when it is time to move or rest. We trust ourselves and the universe in new ways.

Those who have come this far usually now abandon rigid planning. Responding flexibly to situations as they arise becomes important, although this must be balanced with the need to fulfill commitments. A new provisional attitude enters human relationships. People become attuned to moving with the flow, responding to internal needs rather than to external dictates. As this phase continues, people spend less time *making* life happen and more time listening for cues. When closed doors are encountered, they don't try to force anything or to win. Instead, they go a different direction or wait. They become alert to constant opportunity and have the willingness to entertain new ideas. Living one's life can take on the quality of watching a fascinating picture show unfold. Some things you can see far ahead; some events seem to come in from left field.

13. The lessons go on; "the next" is provided

Despite this rosy picture, the lessons go on. If we expect to be "enlightened," our learning will be on-going and relentless. During the later years of the cycle, it often appears that what is required is "mastery" of things left undone in order to move forward with one's unique purpose. One educator, for example, felt more than ready for a job change after years of work on herself. She made repeated attempts to move out of her current position.

Only when she took on the tasks of getting her personal finances in order, however, did she begin to see that a new professional calling was premature until she finished this financial clean-up. Another man realized that his body was the last area of mastery; he needed to quit smoking and lose weight. Exercise had already been instituted.

As one becomes more and more attuned to the inner voice, we are also granted constant lessons that "the next" step in life or love or work will be provided. The unfolding of my business, for example, was a constant revelation of "next steps" being presented. There were long periods of waiting in between and many lessons along the way, but the unfolding occurred as if the universe knew much better than I did what was required and when. Knowing that "the next" is provided requires constant listening for the cues, constant faith during the bare times and letting go of the old ways of forcing anything.

COPING STRATEGIES
1. Take time to become centered

Shifting to a new level, such as that attained during the last phase of midlife growth, takes an enormous amount of energy. Often the body needs time to catch up with the emotional and spiritual shifts. Taking time during this phase to become centered is definitely wise.

How practical it is to "lie low" in order to become more balanced will vary with individuals; not everyone has either the need or the luxury to drop back or out. We need not totally withdraw, however, but instead can make choices about certain demands in our lives in order to encourage the centering/ balancing. One man undertook Rolfing sessions in order to help his body catch up with five years of emotional work. Another took a sabbatical. Unfortunately, we lack affordable drop-out centers as well as societal permission to retreat there. We need more acceptance of how essential these "time outs" from family or jobs can be in consolidating our growth gains.

2. Don't be dismayed by minor regressions

Susan had made considerable headway over the last seven years. As she settled into her new job, she thought she was free at last of the morbid depression that had plagued her life. Then she fell into another blue funk. It came over her so gradually that she didn't recognize it until a friend pointed out how much she was sleeping.

Instantly Susan recognized what was happening. Her approval-seeking behavior with a new boyfriend was mostly the cause. At first she was angry with herself, disappointed that she had fallen back so easily into "the duck soup" as she called it. Would she never stop wallowing in periodic despair, she wondered? Nonetheless, Susan identified her emotional state and its causes very quickly this time. She took immediate steps to extricate herself. Within weeks the gray dullness had lifted.

Much of what we need to remember as we seemingly slide "backwards" in our learning is that we are our own worst critics. Too often we don't give ourselves credit for the progress made. Our standards are different now because we know at later stages much more about what true mental health really means. Losing it, if only momentarily, feels especially harsh because we know how good things can be. The most important thing to remember about seeming regressions is that your response time, from noticing something amiss to climbing out of the pit, is probably greatly reduced from what it was before. If you seem to be learning the same lessons over again, the one big difference is that you are becoming aware much faster. Thus, you can take corrective action much sooner.

3. Dark night of the soul

There may be a point, in later years of the cycle, when we become severely tested about the revelations that have occurred in the last third of our journey. Nothing is happening or moving. In 1989 my usual spring energy surge was replaced by just the opposite. Everything I'd been pursuing in the last several years, including this book and the new business, seemed dead-ended. Consequently, I second-guessed all my decisions about following my path. These were six weeks of the grayest period yet. My self-esteem was at an all-time low. The despair felt extreme; I especially needed a larger purpose in order to feel fulfilled. At the bottom of the abyss, I came to the conclusion that only the love in my life mattered anyway; if books and business were not in the cards, then loving a few others and doing a routine job well would be enough. In fact, love was all that mattered.

Another friend went through a similar test. His symptoms were uncannily like mine, although aggravated by health problems. Brugh Joy also addresses this issue of being severely tested. Joy is an M.D. who helps people with growth through an understanding of the seven chakras, or energy centers in the body. He says that inner growth is a process of becoming "...Christed, and there are dangers about becoming imbalanced as we uncover this divinity." "What really matters," he says, "is your response to *powerlessness*." Both my friend and I had been reduced to exactly that.

Evelyn Underhill *(Mysticism)* calls this passage "the dark night of the soul." Many people mistakenly term some of the earlier stages, when there is plenty of darkness, as the "dark night." In Underhill's classic study of mystics, however, it appears as one of the very last trials to be overcome. It is a time when all the hard-won vision, purpose and meaning is now taken away. We are left with genuine darkness. Another explanation is that here we face our final detachment. Ironically, after we have found new purpose through all the previous work, we are required to let go even this illumination. Such a stripping, however, helps assure that we will not become addicted to the new mission. Rather, we must be willing to be guided by the wisdom of the universe.

4. Don't be disappointed if your experience is less dramatic

Only further research will tell us who does and does not experience Kundalini rising, or the energy surges and cosmic consciousness. The Spiritual Emergence Network found that people who meditate regularly are likely candidates, yet I suspect that other factors are also at work. Those who are highly introverted and intuitive, for example, may be more likely to be tossed into the Maelstrom. In addition, some people may merely have personalities that lie closer to the unconscious.

5. Keep working on yourself

Wanting to be "finished" with this work was an attitude that I carried for much of the journey. It is part of the "perfection syndrome" that I still battle. What seems true, however, is that in some sense one is never finished; staying balanced, healthy and centered is a life-long challenge. Nonetheless, once I left the intense work of the acupressure bodywork therapy, I thought I didn't need more professional help. When I found myself in another muddle, however, a friend suggested massage therapy. That proved to be the tool that facilitated the last several years of growth.

During these later years I no longer delved into painful memory flash-backs as before. Yet when conflicts arose or when I was attempting to clear the more subtle, deeply ingrained patterns in my system, the masseuse's skilled hands and loving wisdom made the difference. In addition, the massages were a way to nurture myself. Now I keep the appointment faithfully because massage is a wonderful way to improve circulation and flexibility; it is an excellent preventative health practice.

6. "Ground yourself" if energy infusions occur

Now that I have been through several periods of energy surges, I am more aware of what to do. In addition to just letting the infusions run their course, knowing that life will be abnormal for several weeks, I know from experience that it helps to ground myself when the energy feels particularly strong. This means I take baths, walk a lot, swim, use the Jacuzzi and ask for lots of hugs. Anything that puts me in touch with the earth and with other human flesh is helpful when the adrenaline starts pumping. Since dietary changes also fluctuate during such surges, I have learned to pay attention to bodily needs. During one episode I went through streaks of cravings for milk, oranges, and sugar. I satisfied those urges, plus there were several days of needing triple my intake of water.

Anyone who is in the midst of puzzling, disturbing, uncomfortable or perhaps frightening infusion periods should consider seeking sympathetic professional help. Reading about the phenomenon can also be an enormous comfort. In addition to describing this experience in depth, Emma Bragdon's book, *The Call to Spiritual Emergency,* has a closing chapter on "How to Help book, *The Call to Spiritual Emergency,* has a closing chapter on "How to Help in a Spiritual Emergency." This resource would be an excellent one to share with friends or family. Some people experience symptoms that require daily living chores to be taken over by others. Another helpful compilation of selections, in *Spiritual Emergency: When Personal Transformation Becomes A Crisis,* has been assembled by Stanislav and Christina Grof.

7. Integrate your learning

Taking the time to integrate your learning is one of the supreme pleasures about personal growth. Some people reread their journals to understand how and in what ways they have changed; others read voraciously or write books. Some develop workshops to share their learning; others merely talk a lot with friends or in discussion groups in order to find meaning in their experience. Whatever the forms you choose, it is important to take the time to integrate the learning. Understanding the process through which we have moved solidifies the changes within us; assigning meaning to the saga provides a rich source of satisfaction about life so far. The chances are also good that people who have fully integrated their learning become beacons of light and inspiration for others.

8

Guidelines
for Self-Discovery:
A Flexible Approach

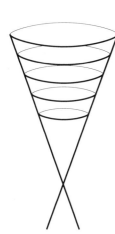

During the '90s many people will likely be plunged into turmoil-filled growth. How will they find their way through the maze? Today many personal growth methods appear offbeat, foreign or downright kooky. Some approaches may be dangerous in the hands of the unqualified. Rolfing, massage therapy, Jungian analysis, meditation, dreamwork, breath work, rebirthing, 12-step programs, yoga, past-life regressions, biofeedback, chakra psychology, Feldenkrais, acupressure, hypnosis, Gestalt therapy and vision quests—These are just some of the methods being proposed. How is the initiate to choose from among a dazzling, sometimes questionable spectrum? Which ones make most sense?

Unfortunately, there are no easy answers. The fact that there are many paths available, however, is an advantage to the seeker, for everyone is unique and usually requires multiple tools. There is, however, no one "right" method. Instead, each person needs to assume responsibility for conducting the journey with the resources and the techniques that work best for them.

How Individual Differences
Affect the Experience

The first thing that is helpful to know when searching for the right tools is that the experience can differ dramatically from one person to another. Like any road map, the description of the stages should be used as a guide, not a rigid prescription. How the destination is reached depends both upon the traveler and the means of transportation; what you see and feel along the way depends upon numerous factors.

The severity with which a person experiences inner change can vary a great deal. Some people, for example, may be only vaguely aware that a process of personality restructuring is underway. Others may be plunged so deeply inward that they can barely function in the outer world, especially during the middle phase. How long the process actually takes and whether blockages can lengthen the time required is also uncertain. One manager, for example, thought her midlife crisis had begun at age 39. At 51 she was finally experiencing rebirth; she had a new job and a zestful outlook on life. The latter emerged full force after a weekend workshop where she fully grieved the death of her parents as well as the departure of her grown children. Genuine renewal had been delayed until she completed this emotional release.

At what age is it usually "normal" to begin this reconstruction of the self? That too is unclear. Late 30s appears to be a common time for initiation, but some men seem to undertake it later, especially in the late 40s and early 50s. The age at which we begin may be related to what else is going on in life. Having child rearing responsibilities, for example, may mean you take on this work in your 40s or 50s rather than earlier.

Another unknown is what might be the relationship between "recovery" as it is known in the addictions treatment field and the psychic growth of midlife. (Recovery is the term that describes both short and long-term addiction treatment paths, including 12-Step groups.) Quite possibly the recovery phase can occur entirely separate from the readjustment of deep personal change as was the case with a counselor. She spent three years in therapy and AA groups coming to terms with her drinking and family incest. Only as she neared 40 did she feel the loneliness so characteristic of the first phase of inner growth. Presumably, she will pass through the maturation experience without the extreme agony that some feel because she has already done considerable healing work.

Another woman realtor, however, felt that deep midlife changes occurred in tandem with recovery. She received no formal addictions treatment, but she utilized rebirthing, workshops and breath work to deal with inner wounds. As she did so, her addictions fell away. Clearing up the confusion about the relationship between recovery and transformation will be a key to successful treatment in the future.

The severity of the experience, or how conscious one is of the phases, stages and characteristics, depends upon a number of personal variables: 1) the degree of trauma in your background, 2) your personal sensitivity level, 3) your ability to support what emerges, 4) your therapist or guide's growth, 5) your personal framework, such as religious or psychological training, and 6) gender differences.

1. The degree of trauma in your background. Those most severely wounded by dysfunctional family situations are more likely to have to work harder at this process. The more abuse received, the more one must return to the sources to heal. There may, however, be a positive side to this truth; the severe dysfunction also serves as a strong motivator. Being more damaged means you apply yourself more fully. As Chinese wisdom suggests, "the more difficult one's parenting, the stronger one's soul."

2. Your personal sensitivity level. People vary considerably in their emotional sensitivity levels, just as we vary in our tolerance to physical pain. One person may register an event with great feeling while another is unaffected. Margaret, a marketing manager from an alcoholic family, knew she was ultra-sensitive. She reacted to everything in her background. That sensitivity, however, may also have had something to do with the role she played in the family. As its youngest member, she became the primary recipient of many unexpressed emotions. She was the "dumpee," in other words, upon whom the rest projected their unconscious feelings.

3. Your ability to support what emerges. Our ability to support what comes up during the stages seems related to two factors. One is an internal dynamic, or the personal courage to face difficult and painful material. But another factor affecting this courage may be the degree of support present in your life. Having supportive friends or family, for example, or access to therapy, makes a difference in how deeply we might be willing to plunge. The woman who experienced renewal after 12 years attributed her breakthrough to the high quality workshop she attended. The safety and trust generated by the counselors provided conditions that allowed deep grieving. Perhaps she was not ready internally to finish the work of an earlier stage until then; but perhaps the right opportunity had not been available to do this intense emotional work any sooner.

4. Growth level and skills of your therapist or guide. Cathy was involved in group therapy for several years. During that period she worked through the bitterness of a divorce. As she continued, however, she felt frustrated with her male therapist. He was telling her that she "should" be getting better by this point. But for her the process was just beginning to deepen. The more that she raised her puzzling feelings, the more didactic he became. Eventually she switched both therapist and methods in order to continue her progress.

Cathy's stumbling block was due to the fact that the therapist himself had not experienced deeper levels of growth. If a helping professional has not done their own in-depth work, they cannot travel with you to the source of your wounds. Kubler-Ross calls this "having our buttons pushed" as professionals. It means that the patient or client's urges toward growth can threaten the therapist enough to trigger a significant blockage. Thus, those with neither the theoretical framework nor the personal experience to support you on the journey may inhibit growth. Inappropriate responses from a helping professional can include explanations that don't fit, faulty diagnoses, prolonged confrontation or analytical meandering. All add up to wasted time and money as well as considerable frustration. Skill level, of course, also varies widely among therapists; at certain points you may need someone with more experience, greater depth or simply a different approach.

5. Your personal framework. The background that we bring to the experience can also influence our consciousness of the process. Those with psychological training, for example, may be more aware because they've been trained to be aware of internal states; they have conceptual understandings that help make sense of things. Similarly, those with strong religious or literary backgrounds may apply that framework. The language, concepts and metaphors in our background affect the way experience is interpreted.

6. Gender factors. The stages involved in becoming a mature person are applicable to both males and females. We don't know for sure what the subtle differences might be, but there are some distinctions. As Robert Bly *(Iron John)* suggests, women may be better at acknowledging their pain and moving into it. Men, by comparison, have a harder time finding their grief. (This is one of the reasons why Bly advocates that men need to do their work in all-male groups.) A woman's inward thrust may also occur more easily because her self is closer to the soul, as some Jungians suggest. Women, however, may have more rage in general because our society has so devalued the feminine. Men also suffer from the social stigmas that it is "unmanly" to ask for help; they experience more social isolation and have poorer relationship skills. The recent growth of the men's movement is doing much to help overcome these deficiencies. As more women and men undergo deep personal change, we may understand better what the underlying differences are, if any.

The Power of Commitment

One of the basic principles behind midlife growth is often overlooked. In many self-help books the impression is frequently given that transformation is "easy." Actually the process is often hard work; as the hero's journey suggests, there are many trials. Getting through it depends a great deal upon your commitment to yourself. Such commitment usually strengthens over time, yet there are critical moments of choice. At such times, having a core value, such as "to thine own self be true," helps remind us what the journey is about and that it is worthwhile.

General Guidelines

The fact that there is no one right path or method means a confusing array of choices. On the other hand, such diversity helps assure that individual needs can be met and that no one path becomes a "hero worship" cult. Whatever your choices, the following guidelines apply:

1. Accept personal responsibility; make this a journey of discovery. Being plunged into pain or crisis is never welcome; accepting it as an opportunity for learning, however, does much to ease the way. Rather than fighting the so-called "negatives" that emerge, for example, such as restlessness, fear or despair, one can welcome these as useful signals. Denying our discomfort is probably normal, yet the sooner we stop fighting the process, the faster we begin to use everything that happens as information for self-knowledge.

2. Know that there is an end. While self-knowledge is a lifelong journey, it is nonetheless important to know that the more painful episodes don't go on forever. Positive outcomes do occur if you keep going and do thorough work. Fear can be expected to usher in each new stage, causing us to question our courage and commitment; seeming regressions can try our patience to the utmost. Such potential setbacks, however, are actually the cyclical process at work, causing us to do the work at ever-deeper levels. The presence of fear warns us that something important is happening. Fear can be our friend when we see it as something that helps us prepare. What is most important about the darkest hours, however, is that things *do* get better. Inner peace, balance and renewed purpose await those who persevere.

3. Reach for help. Deep personal change requires periods of aloneness to distill the events in our lives, but it is not meant to be undertaken without support. Indeed, the quality of your experience may depend upon the nature of the help you find. Both friends and professionals qualify as "helpers." No one should consider it a weakness to reach for such help. There are several cautions about seeking help, however. One is that the ultimate guide or guru you choose must be yourself. Another is that there is also a time to let go of external professional help.

4. Appreciate your tears. Too many of us suffer from ungrieved losses, whether we are Vietnam veterans, children of the ghetto or middle-class adults. This is because growing up itself required swallowing much that hurt. Midlife is the time to surface the hurts and sadness. Being embarrassed about strong feelings, however, will hinder us, for the passage is partly about becoming vulnerable again. In order to become conscious, we must open ourselves to the feelings that we never allowed ourselves as children. Thus, learning to cry again may be important. Tears release negative energy and help cleanse us.

5. Make your own choices. The techniques or approaches that work for one person may not work for another. You should therefore be vigilant about making the choices that fit best for you, regardless of what "the experts" or your friends say. The fact that meditation is a useful tool, for example, means that it sometimes is advised as essential by various teachers. Doug Boyd, however, author of *Rolling Thunder* and friend of yogis, suggests that meditation can actually be dangerous for some people. Kubler-Ross said it just never worked for her. Others swear by it.

Among some of the more alarming growth methods are those involving group processes in weekend seminars or workshops. Some of the techniques used are suspect; if they are used by untrained people they can be unethical and dangerous. Often there is strong pressure to recruit one's friends or to take the "advanced" seminars. One of the most bothersome things about some groups is the pressure put upon participants to conform to the group process. People can be swayed, for example, into revealing more than they really want to share through subtle group norms; such processes may also unleash aftereffects that the facilitator fails to equip people to handle.

The point is that each of us must make our own choices about methods, practices and teachers. Sampling many methods may be interesting and beneficial, but you should not hesitate to say either "yes" or "no" to any particular experience or doctrine. Only you can be the judge of what fits and works for you.

6. Trust yourself. Learning to trust your inner self is one of the sought-after outcomes of maturation. In this case the admonition is meant as reinforcement for *how* you undertake the process; in other words, respect your particular pace. Trust that you will choose the methods or experiences that are right for you, or even that you can learn from a choice that does not fit; trust that none of us is given more than we can bear; trust that there is meaning in your unique experience. Trust especially that there is no one right way.

7. Listen for "faint" messages. Often the directions for next steps are only vaguely audible beneath the surface. This is why such techniques as keeping a journal are effective. They help us pay attention, to listen to the things that our rational minds might otherwise dismiss. Pursuing the safe route is seldom synonymous with growth, and we must often nurse new directions into being.

8. Take time to process. Mary attended an incest survivors workshop in California one week. She decided not to visit a friend afterwards because she knew she would need time to absorb the experience. Even getting back to her job as an administrative aide the next week was difficult. The wounds were so raw and the rage so deep that she needed rest and gentle reflection time. She took plenty of time to be alone and to rest upon return. A month later Mary was much stronger than she had ever been before. She was ready to move on in her therapy, and she was considering going back to school.

Sometimes the need to assimilate is related to an intense emotional experience. At other times the need to let something percolate through us is related to the particular stage of growth. Later stages, for example, are important times to reflect back on where you've come, what you've learned and what the journey means. Sometimes the plateau between one stage and another is the time to make an assessment, as though we pause and gasp for breath before going deeper. Unfortunately, the fact that society does not yet recognize this vital psychological passage means that we lack retreat facilities, "drop-out" centers, "time out" periods and the encouragement to use them as temporary refuge.

9. Don't try to "figure it out." Moving through the stages can feel chaotic because of its cyclical nature, its length and intensity, its unconscious or invisible aspects and its highly individual variations. In a very real sense we all probably muddle through this death-rebirth experience with considerable confusion and disorder. Yet "muddling through" may be exactly what is required. Inner growth is not something that we learn how to do. Instead, it is something that we learn to *accept* and to *allow* with increasing grace and ease. Trying to "figure it out" therefore defeats the purpose. Using our intellect, in fact, can be just one more form of control when giving up control is one of the biggest lessons.

10. Beware of spiritual arrogance. Daniel had been a successful entrepreneur and public speaker. The last six years, however had involved a major readjustment as he found his spiritual path. Along the way he became convinced that he had the keys to helping others be their "majestic selves." Daniel had pure motives and good intentions, but he couldn't see his own arrogance. Even his choice of words was overdone. A know-it-all attitude remained in place. Nowhere in his prescription was there room for the nonmajestic self of the human who has physical, emotional, intellectual *and* spiritual components. Furthermore, he thought that his way was "the" way.

One of the biggest dangers about developing any new system of beliefs, such as we are doing today, is that the new framework becomes a substitute for the old. Thus, instead of moving from external authority to true internal guidance, we exchange one set of beliefs for another. Young people, for example, who have been raised in rigid religious structures and then become disillusioned, may be vulnerable for a time to another set of equally rigid beliefs. Many adults adopt a particular doctrine without tempering it with their own interpretation. So strong is the need within us to be led rather than to accept personal responsibility that we are vulnerable to simplistic answers or charismatic teachers. Almost any teaching can be used as the new external "should" rather than as a tool for internal growth. Even the best of ideas and the most talented of teachers can be guilty of such arrogance.

Beware, then, of too much certainty, of anyone who does not encourage individual choice, and of those who mouth the words without backing them up with action. Be especially wary of anyone who suggests that you should associate only with people who share a particular belief. This is dangerous arrogance. But beware also of your own arrogance. Especially after you have come through the later stages, it is easy to become overly impressed with yourself.

11. Use multiple resources. In addition to the fact that there is no one "right" path or method, it is advisable to use a variety of resources. Workshops may complement individual therapy or vice-versa; a discussion group or lecture can help put pieces into place or be the catalyst for further work; reading may not interest you during some phases while it does at others. One form of therapy may be helpful in the first phase, but second phase work may require something stronger; third phase may lend itself to the things that help physically balance you, such as the martial arts or massage.

12. Develop self-nurturing activities. Learning how to take care of ourselves in new ways is much of what we need to learn during deep personal change. Becoming more whole, in other words, means becoming aware of our needs, then being able to get them met in healthier ways than before. Developing specific self-nurturing activities to help you through the long process, however, may be vital to survival. One woman, for example, became somewhat fanatic about her bath time three times a week. This was the self-pampering time that helped keep her sane. Similarly, she was faithful about a weekly luncheon date with a friend and a monthly long-distance call to another to share up-dates. Each of us needs to develop the routines and rewards that help us weather the rough spots.

Especially after there have been major energy shifts or breakthroughs, you are likely to need extra rest and quiet time. It is not uncommon to feel the need to take special care of yourself for several weeks or months at various times.

13. Beware of pitfalls and sidetracks. There are numerous hazards to growth. One of the most common is to dwell too much on the past and how it formed you. There is a thin line between becoming conscious of our conditioning and the tendency to over-analyze the "why." Analytical understanding by itself is not enough.

Similarly, some groups become stuck on complaints and blame. Various Vietnam veteran support groups, for example, have been accused of this trap. They fail to move to deeper levels either because they lack professional facilitation or else they are unwilling to give up their victim status. Some AA, Al-Anon or other support groups are also afflicted by various strains of faulty group process.

One of the trickiest pitfalls is to know when a situation truly isn't right for you and when it is fear that holds us back from moving forward. When in doubt, check out additional sources for more information, but also challenge yourself. Ask, "Am I avoiding something because I'm afraid to go further?" Our denial systems are so strong that we naturally avoid the deeper levels of pain. This is why the presence of a therapist, friend or compassionate group can be so helpful. We are more likely to dare to risk that pain when support and encouragement are present.

14. Be prepared for "unexpected" consequences. The tales of inner growth are littered with personal stories of people who left behind friends, spouses, children, jobs, careers and locations. Sometimes the painful separation process means saying goodbye to those not interested in growing. Unfortunately, signing up for self-discovery contains no guarantees about security or comfort. If it is clear that people or places need to be left behind, take time for mourning. Remember that whenever you do what you need to do to take care of yourself, you automatically benefit others, even if it does not look that way to them at the time. This does not suggest being callous or selfish about the leaving, but sometimes your leaving is what catalyzes their growth. It is also possible that contact can be reestablished later at a different level that allows you to be yourself. Sometimes, however, it cannot.

Another unexpected consequence is the experience of voids or vacuums. These are periods when it seems as though nothing is moving or happening. These fallow periods are among the most difficult to live with because we are so used to action and movement. Be assured, however, that growth is usually brewing beneath the surface and will emerge when it is time. Learning to accept these quiescent times is part of accepting the feminine within us, including the rhythms and cycles of nature. In nature there is constant ebb and flow, but our masculine-adapted society means that we are uncomfortable with inaction. Sometimes, however, you must be content with feeling dull, uninterested and uninspired. Prolonged depression, however, is something else.

15. Work toward self-forgiveness and self-love. At the heart of the growth process is the enhanced ability to love more fully as a whole person. Sometimes forgiveness of others is not possible, but it is terribly important that we learn to forgive ourselves. There need be no forgiveness when we uncover false guilt or shame. These are the messages received that we were somehow wrong or not enough. Only grieving and righteous indignation can overcome such tapes. But sometimes the "darkness" we uncover may be our own, whether from sexual indiscretions, dishonest acts or outright harm inflicted on others. As we shed light on this "evil" side of human nature, claiming our fair share, the key is to remember that we must forgive ourselves if we are to ultimately grow up. Compassion for others thus starts with ourselves.

A Muddled Treatment Picture

Most people pursuing deep personal change are doing so without benefit of a guiding therapeutic paradigm. As this book's Introduction pointed out, the theory behind this difficult life transition has not been clearly spelled out. Consequently, we lack a coherent community of helping professionals to guide us. The treatment landscape of mental health professionals and spiritual teachers contains an enormous amount of muddle. The reason for this confusion is that we are still in a period of paradigm upset. The process of reformulation means both problems and opportunities for professionals and the lay people who seek their guidance.

Many spiritual teachers, for example, lack an understanding of psychology; they may impose practices on followers who are unready for such development. As teachers, they may be unable to handle neuroses or psychoses. Some groups can be downright harmful as they substitute spiritual tyranny for the patriarchal. On the other hand, many psychologists don't understand the spiritual dimension and may be ill-equipped to travel with their clients to these levels.

Even within the psychotherapy community best equipped to deal with transpersonal levels there are problems. Jungian analysis, for example, may be better prepared theoretically to deal with the unfolding inner psyche. Jung's theories match the discoveries from consciousness research and psychedelic research most closely. Jungian approaches, however, usually don't incorporate body work into their methodology, and there is strong evidence that physical release is often essential. Some experiential therapies, on the other hand, that do include the physical, lack the theoretical foundation about the transpersonal. Thus, clients may have powerful physical releases but lack the means to integrate the experience intellectually. Therapists who conduct workshops may not prepare participants adequately for what to expect later. In addition, many practitioners of nontraditional therapy modes (i.e., Jin Shin, polarity integration, rebirthing, etc.) are unable to explain why or how their methods work; some gifted healers are simply inarticulate.

A more serious problem exists when healers indiscriminately apply a particular technique without having the proper background. But just how you obtain that background is *the* problem, for the old scientific framework upon which psychiatry, psychology and even medicine itself was founded, is now inadequate. New standards, however, have yet to be established. Only a few places, such as the Institute of Transpersonal Psychology in California, have developed a comprehensive training program that includes body work, group methods, individual therapy, intellectual study and spiritual work in their curriculum. During the current transition period in history, when old frameworks are being dismantled and new ones are being assembled, it is often difficult to know where to turn for competent help.

Finding Help To Do This Work

The following suggestions may prove useful:

1. Check out available resources. Ask others for recommendations; attend guest lectures; do some research and reading about various techniques or practitioners before you leap. If you live in a major city, check the weekly "throwaway" newspapers for articles and advertisements about nontraditional healers and workshops.

2. Interview potential therapists or workshop leaders. When you approach a helping professional, find out where that person is in their own growth; insist on knowing something about their training, their background and their methods before submitting to treatment. Any therapist should be willing to conduct an interview without charge as part of an introductory visit. No competent professional would be threatened by a client asserting this right. Many workshop leaders provide preview sessions. Most of all, evaluate whether or not you trust this person and feel good about the rapport. Remember that it is often the quality of the interaction between therapist and client that matters most. The specific techniques they use are merely tools that will be ineffectual without the right relationship.

3. Trust your own instincts. Even if your best friend recommends a specific workshop or therapist, remember that only you can decide. Fads abound in the field of healing and spirituality, and you should be wary of group or peer pressure.

4. Look for methods that match your level of growth. The problem with advising someone to look for methods that match where they are in the process is that nowhere is there a clear guide about which of the many competing schools fit which levels. Only the simplest conclusions can be made, such as that psychoanalysis can help us deal with our personal past and the earlier stages, but it is practically useless for dealing with deeper levels.

The issue is not so simple as matching layers of the psyche with various methods that might correspond to each. Each school, each major theorist and each set of techniques has made contributions to the total picture; each may also miss important pieces. We need to rewrite the textbooks around an integrated approach. There is a need to synthesize information about the levels of consciousness, the stages of growth and the eclectic methods available to help us through them.

5. Consider "mind" versus "body" approaches. So far we know very little about why one approach may work for one person and be totally inappropriate for another. Did one woman's aversion to mental approaches, for example, stem from the fact that she was an intuitive type (according to Jung's theory of types) with a weak sensate side? Thus, maybe she needed physical approaches, such as Gestalt, acupressure body work and massage, in order to develop the sensing side. But perhaps she also gravitated to physical methods because her wounds were severe. She needed methods that would reach deep within the body.

The fact that our developed Western world is such a rational, head-oriented culture may mean that we need considerable help in becoming grounded in our bodies. Techniques such as Feldenkrais, Rolfing, shiatsu, Jin Shin, the Alexander technique, polarity integration, massage, bioenergetics and Gestalt may gain new respectability when we understand the depths of the negative patterns embedded within our physical structures. In addition, the various experiential group approaches based upon sound experience, such as holotropic breath work or Kubler-Ross' "externalization of feelings" workshops, help people do the work of the deeper levels. The limitation of various talk therapies and analysis, or even meditation, is that they do not touch the imprint of some mental patterns that have become embedded in our very cells and bone structures (Wilber, 1977, p. 256).

Most of these nontraditional therapy approaches, with their reliance on pain release, also indicate that there is something drastically wrong with a medical model that aims at killing or controlling pain. The experience of deep personal change instead suggests that we need to find ways to experience and release it. Doctors today are bewildered by the number of chronic pain cases they see and don't know how to treat. "Pain management" has become a

medical buzzword of sorts, yet nowhere is there indication that we need to
enliven pain rather than deaden it in order to reduce it. In addition, those who
suffer from depression and anxiety are often treated only with drugs. The
unfortunate conclusion is that our reliance on the medical model ends up
preventing people from pursuing a normal, natural process that is vital to
attaining emotional health and wisdom.

6. **Consider the causes behind blockages when choosing methods.**
During a workshop in 1984, Dr. Arnold Mindell proposed some interesting
thoughts on why people block the information essential for individuation or
becoming whole. At the top of the list is fear or terror of the information.
Therefore, we don't allow it to emerge. Diseases or symptoms may be full of
information in that they reflect our blocked awareness. Below the symptoms
of cancer, for example, may be our buried rage at parental injustices. Emotional repression, in other words, may produce disease.

Another reason for blocking is self-hatred, or lack of trust in our own
perceptions, suggests Mindell. Unconsciously, for example, we may have
accepted parental admonitions that we "shouldn't" feel angry, sad or hurt, or
that we are bad or wrong for doing so. Therefore, when the strong emotions
come up, we push them back again because that is what we were forced to do
as children. Allowing them to come out simply creates too much of a double-
bind for us to accept.

Still another reason to suppress information is that raising it would cause
an identity crisis of some kind. Perhaps it would face us with a career change,
for example, a geographical move or a change in relationship partners. Any
of these could pose such a threat that we are unwilling to deal with our inner
truth. The final reason, suggested Mindell, is that the signal may be too weak
and is not picked up. This is another reason why body work and experiential
approaches may be particularly important. They amplify weak signals
(Mindell workshop, Denver, CO, July 1984).

Given the reasons for blocking the process, there is every indication that
rigorous methods are necessary. Plenty of courage is also essential. You must
be committed to finding and becoming your very best self.

Specific Self-Help Tips

In addition to the *attitudinal* guidelines and external methods you
choose to do your work, the following self-help tips are offered as a summary
list:

1. Keep a journal; do not worry about form or content, but do be sure it's
private. Record feelings, dreams, insights, questions.

2. Reread the journal to assess progress and integrate learning.

3. Find a support or study group, such as Adult Children of Alcoholics
(ACOA), Edgar Cayce explorations, a spiritually oriented group, etc. Recognize the difference, however, between a support group and therapy group. The

latter should be staffed by a trained professional; it offers a deeper experience than mere support or encouragement of growth.

4. Create a support group if you can't find one.

5. Talk to friends.

6. Commit yourself to at least a trial period of therapy.

7. Find a 12-step program, such as AA, Al-Anon, Overeater's Anonymous, Gambler's Anonymous, etc. Use it as a set of mental attitudes and discipline that helps you through the stages.

8. Seek help from a treatment center for substance abuse, co-dependency, or sexual addictions treatment if necessary. Many alcoholism and drug centers now have co-dependency units. In these environments some heavy "digging" can occur, plus the support for initial behavioral and attitude changes. Some have out-patient programs.

9. Use visualizations; tape your own from a book and listen to them regularly.

10. Learn relaxation or breathing techniques; use these to calm and quiet yourself, or as prelude to meditation.

11. Write out affirmations, such as "I am peaceful," etc.

12. Try "active imagination." This is a Jungian technique that could be explained by a therapist; John Sanford's *The Invisible Partners* contains a description.

13. Read an inspirational book in a meditative way, namely slowly, thoughtfully, reflectively.

14. Write a letter to someone who has done you an injustice. Don't send it. Save it, burn it or tear it up.

15. Develop a "progress list" full of the intangibles of your growth over the past several years. Celebrate afterwards.

16. Get a massage as a treat.

17. Get regular massages as a way of becoming clear and staying that way.

18. Attend a workshop about some subject that will help you work on yourself, such as dreamwork, intensive journaling, etc.

19. Beat a tennis racquet on the bed when you're feeling angry, or when you suspect you might be.

20. Explore the healing properties of new age music.

21. Develop a personal ritual that helps you with endings. Or develop a ritual that helps you start or end the day.

22. Make time to be alone.

23. Read other accounts of psychological or spiritual unfolding (see References).

24. Read Abraham Maslow's chapter on "Characteristics of the Healthy Personality" from *Motivation and Personality* or the description of "God's Teachers" from the *Course in Miracles*.

25. Learn yoga; do it with a friend or by attending a class.

26. Try a martial art, such as karate or t'ai chi for balance.

27. Sign up for an outdoor experience, such as "Outward Bound" or a ropes course for the psychological breakthroughs it can provide.

28. Try biofeedback.

29. Conduct a "laugh in" with a friend or a larger group if you're particularly down.

30. Buy a stuffed animal that reflects your "inner child." Such props do not belong at work, but at home they can be hugged and slept with, especially when you're feeling hurt, little, vulnerable and unbalanced. Many therapists use such props to help people tap the inner child; both women and men are discovering that having a personal symbol is great comfort.

31. Get regular exercise; eat nutritiously.

32. Finally, if at all possible, don't take yourself too seriously or dwell too much on things. As a therapist/chaplain at a treatment center suggests, people really do know how to do the inner journey. While it may sometimes seem confusing and difficult, it is also a natural process. We should avoid making it seem too mysterious. What most of us need in order to successfully undertake deep personal change is more societal "permission" from those around us, plus some helpful guidance along the path.

9

Rewards
of the Journey:

The Renewed, Creative Person

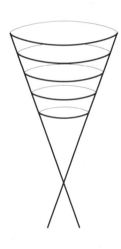

Listening to Elisabeth Kubler-Ross tell stories about her dying patients is anything but gruesome. She is a diminutive, plain-looking woman. She speaks with a thick, Swiss accent; her words of loving wisdom have been earned at the bedsides of so many terminally ill. Immense respect for others permeates her examples of how a cancer patient found peace, how a married couple ended years of hostility, or how a dying child became a teacher to his parents. "It is very clear to me that what we have learned from the dying are lessons for the living," she says. Unexpected creativity, inner peace and spiritual wisdom often grace their lives before physical death if they have cleared themselves of fear, guilt, shame and negativity. "If we could reach this stage of acceptance earlier, says Ross, "we would have far different and more meaningful lives. We would appreciate the small things and have different values."

The Power of Vision

Why haven't we known about these "lessons" before? Is it because we've been so afraid of death in our culture? Our dread of death, however, is only a partial explanation. The unfortunate thing about the modern age is that we have lacked a compelling *vision* of what it means to live "the good and healthy life." Because we've been blinded by the limited view of the patriarchy, because science worship replaced meaningful religion, and because we are encrusted with so much negative upbringing, we have been devoid of models that might inspire us upward. Our self-limited views are implanted early in life.

As Robert Fritz, musician and architect of creativity theory points out, "Much of what you learned growing up was what not to do and what to avoid." Children are rightfully taught limitations essential to their survival. (But they are taught too well.) In one psychological study, children wore tape recorders for several days. When the tapes were analyzed, the psychologists conducting the study found that 85 percent of what had been said to those children concerned either what they could not do, or how what they were doing was wrong. It is no wonder that an underlying impression of powerlessness lives on long after we know how to cross a street or light a match safely (Fritz, 1984, pp. 25-26).

An essential step to overcoming this fundamental belief in our power-lessness is to have a vision that life can be different. Seeing how life can be better helps us make new choices. Up until recent years, we have had only a few portraits of higher human health. Abraham Maslow's studies of the healthy personality, along with Carl Jung's feminine/masculine balance, constitute part of that beacon. Maslow described people who had peak experiences, were involved in a purpose outside themselves, were humorous yet serious and portrayed a host of "abnormal" qualities, such as humility alongside self-confidence. Jung described men who incorporated the feminine side of themselves and women who incorporated their masculine as they matured. The idea that living with opposites is possible in our more developed states was a recurrent theme for both theorists. Jung also developed a theory of types that helps people see the multiple sides of their natures. We differ in how those four sides, thinking, feeling, sensing and intuition, are employed.

The power of Maslow's and Jung's models, or any positive picture of higher human development such as those found in some Eastern religions, cannot be overestimated. The vision acts as a catalyst, much the way that someone who believes in us does. We are spurred onward. During the 1970s these pictures of human health began to be disseminated widely to a professional community of therapists and consultants through the humanistic psychology movement; now transpersonal psychology is pushing the frontiers. The transmission of a new vision of human nature to the broader public remains as unfinished business, along with the incorporation of the vision into daily life and leadership.

Outcomes of Deep Personal Change

Many of the rewards of deep personal change involve subtle, almost imperceptible shifts. The changes occur gradually, over the months and years, snowballing into a larger, cumulative effect. Many of the dramatic, life-altering episodes, such as divorce, death, job loss or other trauma that we face, add up to special turning points. From these experiences we learn important lessons about ourselves and others. It is as if none of us truly matures without challenge and adversity.

The "new person" who emerges creates a tremendously hopeful outlook for the human race. In many ways these women and men will be beyond the corruption of greed and power. Like the saints and philosophers who paved the way, these people have come through a healing experience. They have become capable of new inner direction, and they are actual or potential leaders of others. Such people reflect 1) changes in attitude, values and outlook, 2) changes in behavior and demeanor, 3) changes in health and diet, including stress management, 4) an enhanced quality of life, 5) expanded visionary, creative powers, and 6) a new sense of freedom. Separating these characteristics into categories is somewhat misleading, for the attributes overlap. Nonetheless, for descriptive purposes, the breakdown is useful.

1. Changes in attitude, values and outlook

The heart of psychological maturation is a significant perceptual shift that changes the way people see the world. Part of that change involves the ability to *transcend* situations on a regular basis. Instead of seeing things as pro or con, black or white, for instance, to transcend them means to see the deeper issues, or to understand their meaning beyond the conflict. To transcend means "to rise above" the limits.

The director of a health clinic, for example, was tired of the noisy, nasty abortion debate in his community. He could see that neither side would win their battle. He empathized with the pro-choice people about their concern for women's rights; but he felt the pro-life people also had a case that abortion too often supplanted birth control. The Director, however, saw the real problem as lack of education about contraception. How to prevent unwanted pregnancy was the core issue, not whether one or the other position was right. Arguing the pro-life position versus the pro-choice one was akin to arguing about religion. Instead, he decided to shift the debate to a different level.

Toward that end, the Director invited counselors reflecting both viewpoints to provide services at his clinic. As that innovation took hold, he made "parental education" the focus for his new program; he invited supporters of both positions to join him in throwing their combined resources behind this educational thrust. The Director thus united opposing factions behind a larger goal. By helping the two sides see a common vision and agreeing to honor their differences, he moved the action to a level beyond win-lose.

When one is able to transcend the limits, problems become opportunities and challenges. Issues are examined for larger meaning and hidden benefit. Rigid positions are abandoned in favor of a search to hear out all sides. Diverse viewpoints are all seen as contributions to the whole. People who have gone through deep personal change are more apt to see things optimistically, to look for the new or fresh angle and to approach life with the wisdom and understanding that is beyond "either-or" thinking.

Closely related to the ability to transcend situations is the characteristic of being less judgmental of others. So much of adult growth involves facing our dark sides that afterwards you are more compassionate toward human failings. "There but for the grace of God, go I" is a common reaction rather than judgments, although "tough love" skills are equally valued. High standards are demanded of oneself and others. To help others attain these, however, the mature person exhibits the mixture of support and toughness that brings out the best in another person. Their own hard-won self-acceptance translates readily into more acceptance of others.

Other changes in values and attitudes include a new appreciation for interdependence and "community." People who have been through inner growth often have powerful experiences of feeling fused with nature, other people and life in general. They also realize their need for people in a healthy sense without that being addictive or deficiency-based. This sense of interdependence, that we are all part of the whole, resides alongside deep respect for individual uniqueness. "No man is an island," they would say, while at another level they are comfortable with the fact that each of us is essentially alone. The opposites come together during maturation as two sides of a larger truth that is held comfortably in balance.

The development of a more loving, compassionate nature and a recognition of our interdependence is often behind the desire to be involved in a vision and goals larger than oneself. Ted Turner, the cable TV executive, is one example. Whether or not Turner would identify with the process described in this book is unknown; he has been a controversial man, evoking both intense like and dislike. Turner does, however, admit to being considerably different in his 50s than the brash young man of 40. Today he continually expresses his interest in peace and the environment. He tries to use his networks to better the world. His sponsorship of athletic games is designed not just to make money but also to expand contact among cultures. He also freely admits his previous errors, including selfishness and inattention during a failed 18-year marriage. Whether you like him or not, Turner displays an unusual acceptance of himself.

He also describes himself as an "adventurer." During TV interviews, Turner appears remarkably unaffected by ego; instead, he seems to concentrate on enjoying the journey as much as possible. That apparent lack of concern for ego is one of the most important value changes that emerges from inner change. Not that such people are without ego. In fact, the sense of self-identity within optimally healthy people is very strong. They don't, however, seem any longer to be attached to position, status, power, or acclaim from external sources. Instead, they find validation from within. Much of the reason for this is that maturation involves countless episodes of "letting go" of attachments, whether those are people, emotions, beliefs or money. This does not mean that evolved people don't enjoy money or success; they do, but the trappings become means rather than ends.

The switch from ends to means was dramatically evident in the life of an interior designer who now lives in a plush home in San Diego. Her route there, however, included being uprooted from a marriage to a doctor who had provided a status-rich life in a Los Angeles suburb. Leaving these surroundings, including her golf and Junior League memberships, at first felt like a huge loss. Initially she felt embarrassed, belittled, angry and disoriented. Eventually she accepted the drastic changes as inevitable and made the best of it. Raising two children in a small apartment while she went back to school was not easy. Now, however, she enjoys a promising new career amidst very comfortable surroundings; the difference is that she now knows that neither being a doctor's wife nor material riches are the important things. The designer is no longer attached to the outer trappings because she found inner resources; she nonetheless enjoys what she has created.

2. Changes in behavior and demeanor

Jack had been senior partner in a huge law firm before his marriage broke up. The divorce didn't affect his work, but it initiated many other changes, including a remarriage and the impetus to move beyond the confines of legal work. As he continued his growth through therapy and various workshops, his interpersonal skills improved dramatically. His compassion for others was deepened; people, in fact, felt drawn to him like a magnet. They trusted him instantly, responding to his deep sensitivity and understanding. Ironically, Jack's desire to remain a lawyer waned as his skills and demeanor changed. He had less patience for those mired in interpersonal issues that seemed largely adversarial. As he undertook a career transition to public speaker and author, Jack also decided not to work any more 12-hour days. He was tired of burning the candle at both ends. He wanted a balanced lifestyle with more leisure, family time and hobbies.

Increased sensitivity toward others is a major outcome of renewal. In some ways we may become more patient; we can relax about the timing of things rather than trying always to "make life happen." Yet we may feel less patient about those who are not involved in personal growth. No longer do we "need to be needed," nor to solve situations that seem hopeless. We also become much better about taking care of ourselves; time for rest and regeneration become sacrosanct. Nonetheless, people do not become selfish or egocentric. They become less of both, but they have high regard for themselves. They know they can give their best to a vocation or others only if they know how to nourish and renew themselves.

Perhaps one of the most important changes in behavior that characterizes our now-healthier person is that she or he responds to internal signals rather than external ones. Jack's choices, for example, were a direct result of being more attuned to his inner needs. Gradually he learned to obey rather than deny them. Now he noticed his reactions to situations and made continual adjustments away from the "shoulds" that had previously driven him. Those "shoulds" included ideas about income level, career, long working days and meeting the expectations of others.

Donald Marrs, an ex-advertising executive who described his long transition process in *Executive in Passage,* is another who grew to value the inner voice. Marrs writes of the battle between "the chairman of the board" and the inner voice. The "chairman," of course, stands for the "societal shoulds," the rational side that often speaks in opposition to inner needs or desires. Marrs went through a long process of expending financial resources while he pursued his personal growth. First he wrote a screenplay; later he attempted to switch to film-making. Each so-called "failure," however, led him closer to what he really wanted and needed to do.

Marrs' inner voices were sometimes faint and irrational, but he studiously followed them. Each encounter taught him something that he needed for putting things together in a more satisfying way. Today he heads a marketing firm that services only people and products that he values. Gone are the days of wasting his creativity on cereal ads, gas guzzling cars or tobacco. Those had been the agency accounts in the days when he began his inner journey.

Changes in ethical choices, including sexual behavior are also common. People generally become more interested in intimacy versus sex. They seek partnership with an equal where they can share multiple parts of themselves; monogamy becomes an important aspect of building trust and respect, not just a way to deal with the AIDS epidemic.

Changes in business ethics and values also occur. Mark was a previous "hot shot" broker for an international real estate firm before he underwent such a transition. In the late '80s he had ridden high on the wave of big commissions from business development. He lied about his taxes and played the sales game fiercely. Mark loved his mobile phone, the rush-rush atmosphere and the nationwide trips, not to mention London and Zurich. Then the bottom dropped out of the market. Mark's income dropped to a quarter of what it had been. As he sold the big house, a jeep, and otherwise scaled back, he took stock of who he really was. Several years of painful readjustment went by before Mark realized that his aim was to truly serve his customers. As he matured, he experienced the satisfaction of providing knowledgeable service and meticulous follow-up. Few of the trappings of success mattered as they had before. Now, the things that helped him sleep easily were honest tax returns and fair, everyday tactics.

Almost all of the changes in behavior and demeanor that characterize inner growth can be summed up as a shift to more authentic, game-free behavior. As we become more real to ourselves, more secure and autonomous, we have no need anymore to lie to ourselves, much less to others. Lying to ourselves includes the very human tendency we all have not to know who we really are, including how we might be manipulating others or kidding ourselves. Our defenses often shield us from the truth unless dramatic events help us see more clearly. Through growth, however, our masks and our defenses are stripped bare at deep levels, with the result that we no longer need to pretend or posture.

3. Changes in health, diet and stress

One of the best kept secrets about transformation is that it makes a huge difference in how you handle stress. You sleep more easily at night because worries don't plague you. When you live in tune with your needs, you do not take on too much; you rest and pace yourself because you are aware of inner signals. Things get done with a rhythm that is easy and gentle rather than frantic. When you sense yourself off center, adjustments are readily made. Most importantly, when you are no longer in conflict with yourself because the internal boundaries have been dissolved, you meet life with a calm that affects all choices. Decisions are made more easily, or else they are suspended until "the right time." A sense of equanimity and peace characterizes our nature because we have substituted a whole self for a divided head and heart.

As your energy becomes better balanced throughout the stages, important health changes may be noticed. One woman banker who was affected by debilitating arthritis was cured as she did body work therapy. Her new mental freedom and outward radiance were noticed by customers and colleagues alike. Others report weight losses, allergy and asthma relief and the disappearance of backaches. Bodily realignments can also occur, including spinal adjustments and changes in height or posture.

The mysterious relationship between physical and psychological health has received much attention in recent years. Norman Cousins, diagnosed with a terminal illness, for example, refused to accept the verdict. Instead he watched hours of funny movies and noticed that such "laugh therapy" brought noticeable improvement. Changing our mental outlook may be critical to physical health.

While the painstaking growth involved in deep personal change should not be considered a substitute for medical treatment, the chances are good that changing inner selves will do much to alleviate physical problems. In fact, illness can be a strong message about the need to heal deep, underlying emotional patterns.

Particularly toward the later stages of growth, there are strong urges to eat a lighter diet and to exercise regularly. Poor habits may prove stubbornly resistant to change, but there is almost an inner urge from the body to become and stay healthy. Falling backwards into old habits becomes uncomfortable.

4. Quality of life changes

As our outlooks, behaviors and choices change, and as we move toward the renewal phase of maturation, we notice that the quality of life is improving. The sense of satisfaction ranges from quiet appreciation to outright joy. Our sense of aliveness deepens everything, from viewing a sunset to enjoying work or being with friends.

The quality of personal relationships improves as we develop more capacity for true intimacy. Having found a new relationship with our self, we are better able to join with others in nonaddictive ways. Since there is little need to "hide" anymore, we can truly share ourselves; we can also see and hear others more accurately, with more understanding. We have become sensitive to ourselves and can thus be sensitive to others. Wanting to share our sense of well-being extends to the desire to celebrate in large and small ways when appropriate. A decreased tolerance for superficial events or relationships, however, is also present. We move away from those people who don't meet us at our level, and we may choose fewer but deeper friendships. The need for alone time may actually increase, although there is a willingness to turn outward again after the intense self-reflection.

The fact that people become integrated, balanced personalities has a profound effect on how they live each day. A sense of harmony pervades life. They live more in the moment rather than worrying about the future. Our sense of humor also improves or deepens. The humor, however, is usually based upon finding laughter in the immediate situation rather than in jokes. The need to control things or people has diminished or fallen away, although we still make discerning choices. One loses oneself in the flow of things more often.

5. Expanded visionary, creative powers

One of the most important by-products of deep personal change is the release of untapped creative potential. As the limitations about self are removed and as the energy blockages are cleared, we are able to tap more regularly into our inherent creative power. No longer hindered by negative self-beliefs, we find renewed self-confidence about creating life for ourselves. This includes being imaginative about the way we live, such as cooking or dressing differently and celebrating small things, as well as being more innovative in our careers. During the last stages, strong envisioning episodes may occur that indicate new lifework directions. Creativity is the ability to make up a vision of the new, the better or the beautiful and then take the steps to bring it into form.

People who have come through maturation bring new spontaneity and freshness to almost everything, from dinner conversations to major work projects. They often explore many new avenues, from health habits to hobbies and vocational interests. Life opens up again after the darkness that seemed so long and deep. New horizons appear once we have shed old roles, beliefs and behaviors.

Much of the reason for an improved ability to envision is related to developing our intuition. During the emotional clearing work, the channels are opened within us so that our intuition or inner wisdom can emerge as a major guide. We *trust* this source of knowing more as the emotional filters are removed. The ability to merge inner knowledge with outer thinking grows stronger as we move deeper into the growth process; at times we are able to make new internal connections almost magically. For those who may be highly intuitive by personality type, the clearing can mean that their visionary qualities come to the forefront.

Several companion qualities also emerge. The ability to use everything for learning, for example, affects creativity. The renewed person is apt to believe that "there are no mistakes." There aren't any because they use everything that happens as learning. There is no need to defend being "right" about something or worry about being "wrong;" instead, every event or reaction becomes just another step in receiving information or unfolding a project. This ability to be open to feedback, to continuously make adjustments, means that you become a much more "open system," capable of rapid learning. Being receptive to this input and being willing to adjust, affects both work and play. We are able to be flexible versus rigid; we are able to more easily adapt to incoming changes. There is no longer such a strong investment in hanging on to a position of any kind. Such flexibility and openness also return us to a sense of awe, wonder and curiosity that we once had as children. Healthy people who have matured successfully generally know how to laugh and play with new gusto. Even their language changes to expressions that contain words such as "wow" or "fantastic."

In addition to enhanced creativity and new openness to learning, the renewed person is someone who is likely to be on track about fulfilling their unique purpose. Especially at the later stages, new possibilities open to reveal what you as a person are meant to do to achieve your potential. Joseph Campbell, the expert on mythology, called this "following your bliss." What Campbell meant is the ability to follow those avenues that deeply interest and satisfy us rather than to follow money, status or what someone else thinks we should do or be. Committing ourselves to that unique purpose does not mean that such directions appear magically or that pursuing them is easy. Continually we must make choices to focus and pursue our path. Maturation, however, usually unveils the threads and provides the courage to follow our convictions.

6. Freedom

One of the most underrated but important effects of deep personal change is that it frees us of our negative conditioning. Thus, we become significantly freer of guilt and worry—freer of self-doubts and fear—freer even of time constraints when we live more fully in the moment—and freer of the limits of linear logic when we create wholistically, through a combination of intuition and rational thought.

Becoming a whole person, experiencing the death and rebirth involved in maturation, however, does not mean that "problems" cease or that some magical state of bliss ensues. As the old Zen saying suggests, "Before enlightenment, chop wood, carry water. After enlightenment, chop wood, carry water." In other words the problems that do occur are seen differently; they are more likely to be regarded as opportunities for learning rather than setbacks. Such an attitude means that all of life can be an adventure.

This sense of inner freedom emerges from the hard work of looking both at oneself and at the negative conditioning that formed most of us. The nature of the patriarchy was to be perfectionistic, to instill order and obedience in the child. Most of us grew up as children with a pervading awareness of what we couldn't or shouldn't do. If families were especially dysfunctional because of alcoholism or other abusive patterns, we have special unconscious "programs" to undo. Yet even "normal" families have lived with emotional repression, restricted roles and perfectionistic standards. Such conditions damage wholeness and self-worth. Hence, a huge reservoir of false shame and guilt resides within each of us *unless* we take the inner journey. Only deep personal change can free us of this baggage.

10

Beyond Greed and Power:

Healing the Giant Ego of Business

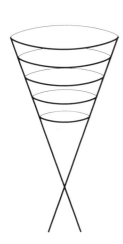

Public confidence in our business and political leadership has declined over the last decade. Outright scandal, outrageous executive compensation, untruths, incompetence and lack of vision have eroded trust. As a consequence, people are asking, uneasily, what will the future be like? Will I have a job? What about health care coverage? Some questions are self-concerned, but people care about others too. How can we solve homelessness, racism, the education crisis, drug and alcohol abuse, the budget deficit, AIDS and crime? Beyond the domestic issues, what about Eastern Europe and the third world?

Raising the questions creates confusion, insecurity, anger and despair. Even adults with strong mental health and money in the bank lose hope and heart. Our society appears on the surface to be in rapid decline, and the leadership in power is either paralyzed or still in denial.

Looking Deeper:
Death Rattles of an Old Era

The confusion of the moment, the sense of losing perspective or hope, can be alleviated somewhat by applying our understanding of growth stages to society in general. In other words, the process of transformation, or deep, fundamental change, is also one that describes how organizations learn and how civilization itself unfolds. And at certain times, such as the present, a restructuring needs to occur.

The same stages that apply to personal change can be seen in society at large. Thus, the end of the cold war, symbolized by the crumbling of the Berlin Wall and the subsequent collapse of communism, ended a global era of uneasy Tension/Confusion/Conflict between superpowers. (Tension/Confusion/Conflict is the inner stage where hopelessness is common, as is lack of movement or feeling stuck. During this period many internal conflicts surface; people feel "at sea.")

Now we are entering a decade of Fear/Guilt/Grief, when the loss of an old civilization needs to be mourned while fragile new forms are nurtured. Our task is nothing less than to restructure the current order. But just as the ego hangs on so tenaciously during deep personal change, so too will we struggle mightily during this decade. The old order, based upon top-down control, and comparable to our ego, does not want to give in to the forces heralding change.

The severity of the struggle comes from the fact that the patriarchy itself is dying, including a set of institutions and beliefs based upon obedience to external authority—principally, "the father." A look at our political, economic, educational and religious organizations leads to the conclusion, as futurist Paul Shay suggested in a keynote speech at the Organization Development Network Conference in 1991, that "organized everything is in trouble." From the Catholic church to the school system, criminal justice, the government and the family, it is apparent that our complex social systems are not solving problems, addressing issues or maintaining the order they once did.

Unfortunately, it is less apparent that it is time for many organizations to "die" so they can be reformed, replaced or reborn; many systems are full of decay, abuse of power and oppression. Too many exist for the convenience of those in control rather than for those they serve. The dying process, however, is never easy or comfortable. The death rattles of the patriarchy promise massive dislocation and personal trauma for many. The more unconscious we remain, the worse it will be. But like it or not, a profound restructuring is stirring across all institutional and organizational life. Such upheaval is similar to the midlife reorganization that occurs in the human psyche. This inevitable growth process can either be subverted or else it can produce profound learning and renewal. The fact that it is happening promises shocks and aftershocks for years.

The upheaval has actually been with us for some time. The leadership vacuum of the '80s, for example, was symptomatic of a "body" that has lost its way. Similarly, the person in deep transition feels adrift, unhinged, lost for a while. Now the highs and lows of Fear/Guilt/Grief are evident. A new self (and a new society) is taking root beneath the surface, but strong, short-lived negative events can also test us severely. Fear/Guilt/Grief is an especially confusing period of personal change. Sensations of impending doom can exist alongside abundance and breakthrough. Feeling connected or fused with others, however, is another hallmark, along with falling apart and losing control.

Such up-and-down episodes can be seen in the mirror of world events. Freedom and democracy, for example, beckon throughout Eastern Europe while economic issues threaten their survival. The collapse of communism unites people at a new level while ethnic divisions tear the Russian empire apart. The Gulf war brought new suffering and carnage, while it reordered the free world and united many in a common bond. The U.S. economy falters alarmingly while technological breakthroughs indicate strong creativity beneath the surface.

At a very personal level, many Americans fear that our way of life is in jeopardy and can never be regained. Some, however, believe that new values and a healthier balance need to replace a heartless, consumer-oriented lifestyle that robs us of the genuine good life. The bad news is that hard times may be upon us; the good news is that it is turning us away from materialism toward basic values.

These are just a few of the examples to illustrate that a new world order is struggling to be born or reborn; it does so, however, amidst significant crumbling and disarray. As the saying goes, "for every act of creation there is one of destruction." There is much birth and death these days, but we particularly feel the pain of a dying culture that has persisted for five thousand years or more. The patriarchy, with its equivalency to our egocentric stage of development, still permeates our thought patterns and our societal and family structures. So strong is the grip of that ego and the patriarchal order that it is hard to see that new values, models and forms are emerging tentatively, like tender shoots, amidst the ruins.

Unprecedented Change = Organizational and Personal Crisis

A number of cultural historians, futurists and pattern-watchers all generally agree that current times are ones of unprecedented change. Other transition periods have also brought upheaval, but never has such rapid change been thrust upon us. The magnitude and speed of this change means that it is truly transformative. Indeed, the awareness that time is running out, that we might have only 10-20 years to solve certain problems, provokes both urgency and panic. Will we have enough time to mend our ways? The outcome remains uncertain.

In the early '90s the effect of all this change on organizations became apparent after considerable denial. Finally, U.S. business began to wake up. We now see that Japanese success can no longer be blamed upon their lower labor costs or their spirit of cooperation. Rather, we must pay attention, belatedly, to *quality*. Becoming competitive in the new global economy is *not* something we can choose to do or not do. We must adapt rapidly to the reality of world markets.

Furthermore, the advent of new technologies, especially information technology, is changing the very way that business is done. Patterns of decision-making, according to the old rules of power, control and authority, are simply obsolete. Neither do the old modes fit the new inner-directed values of employees, who want, increasingly, to control their own lives. Finally, the mind-boggling pace of change means that businesses are being threatened daily with survival. Flexibility, fast reaction and leanness are critical to their existence.

Attempting to cope with all this change is leaving its cruel mark upon many. Both the "haves" and the "have nots" are being affected. During a time when more resources for social problems are needed, paying the interest on the budget deficit cripples our ability to act. The real lack, however, is vision, inspiration and national will. Resources might follow if creativity and commitment were present. In the meantime, poverty is worsening amidst abundance.

At the opposite end of the spectrum, we see executives suffering too. There is fear in their eyes as they realize that a new ball game is afoot and that they are unprepared to play. Furthermore, job loss has hit even them. But it is worse in the ranks. So many middle managers and white collar workers have been let go in the wake of mergers and down-sizing that the lesson has been learned. The lesson is that there *is* no job security any longer. Correspondingly, there is little if any company loyalty. Unfortunately, the tools that might encourage self-reliance and redirection, such as massive adult education and retraining, are not available or seldom sought. Too many continue to believe that "the organization" will provide work. Where is the vision for a new society where education and change will be lifelong? Such a vision means new coping tools for people. Such possibilities require more responsive institutions and a new type of GI bill to support initiative.

For those who do have a job, unwanted leisure is not the problem. Instead, overwork, stress and burnout are common. How ironic that in an age when technology and "progress" was supposed to free us, many people are working longer hours than ever before. Some are on a treadmill because their organization makes demands; some escape consciously or unconsciously into workaholism; still others are stretched to breaking with the load of managing both family and job.

The workplace is still not a very enlightened place to be. Too many businesses are counter-productive, noncreative environments. This is principally because they are being run by unhealthy people who perpetuate dysfunctional norms and practices. Yet even healthier organizations are being socked with unparalleled change that stretches coping mechanisms. Is it any wonder that disenchantment and deep uneasiness accompany us into the 21st century?

Given the forces that are driving us onward (i.e., globalization, new technologies, new values and the pace of change itself), it is perhaps surprising that there is as much resiliency as there is. The resiliency, however, exists, mostly within and among persons, for all institutional/organizational forms are threatened unless renewal processes are undertaken.

The trouble with making that statement is that we still lack a "technology of transformation" for organizations and their leaders. In other words, we don't have a body of theory and practice that shows managers "HOW TO CHANGE" their organizations in deep, fundamental ways. Even when we know that renewal is needed, the tools to reexamine, revision and reform are missing. New tools and a more complete framework are just emerging. Neither do we understand very well how to change ourselves, for organizational change is dependent first and foremost upon personal change.

As with so many other fields that have gone through upset in the last 20 years, so too is a new management paradigm still woefully incomplete. Bits and pieces of it have surfaced in places such as Silicon Valley, some information-based companies or in the cutting-edge work of a few consultants. From such sources we hear about involving people at all levels, of empowering workers, of super-lean management, and of decision-making without hierarchy that employs state-of-the-art information technology. We also read of self-managing teams, trust and openness that is unbelievable by yesterday's standards and the need for bold leadership.

Behind or below this emergent paradigm, however, is a set of attitudes, relationships, behaviors and skills that requires a very different person than the rigidly-defended authority figure that we used to know as leader. This "new person," whether manager or worker, will be essentially beyond greed and power. They will focus instead on *serving* others, or helping people become whole and effective. They will empower people to find and live out their essence and potential.

Interim Band-Aids Still Popular

The push to attain new organizational and self-knowledge, however, will not likely be characterized by immediate wise choices. The early '90s, in fact, may merely be the wake-up call. In the meantime, many organizations are still applying Band-Aids. These temporary solutions fail to remedy the need for underlying, fundamental change that must start in our psyche.

One of the latest improvement programs to be taken seriously is the rush to emphasize *quality* in companies. While the movement is overdue and promises to help make us competitive again, it has some drawbacks. Notably, there is often too much emphasis on statistics and measurement. Instead, effective quality programs require a change in attitude from the top down. Another failing is that companies often seek the latest guru consultants and immediate implementation. U.S. business has a history of seeking external fads and "fixes," whether Management By Objectives or Quality Circles. Furthermore, they want such approaches to work instantly. Long-term commitment, in-depth change and self-critical attitudes have not been characteristic. Instead, the CEO or top team searches for methods to "train or fix" the workers. Management arrogance, and their failure to truly listen and learn, has been both harmful and foolish. Sensitive listening, however, plus appreciation for another's contribution, can only come if you know yourself deeply and are secure enough not to feel threatened.

Only time will tell whether the quality push will make a difference to U.S. business. At its best it could bring revolutionary culture change, with true empowerment for workers and an end to bureaucracy. At its worst there will be millions spent on installations that promise much and deliver little. Already many workers are wary and distrustful of one more program or change strategy.

Some other "Band-Aids" that are being applied include still more mergers, plus the training of more and more Masters of Business Administration (MBA) students who learn obsolete information. During the '80s we saw successive rounds of mergers that were seldom driven by visionary goals. Instead, the purpose of most was short-term financial gain. People and structures were shoved together with little regard for effective change processes or the human costs involved. Such sweeping changes were among the first indications that a societal restructuring was taking place. The restructuring, however, was controlled by a few and carried out with scant regard for long-term consequences.

Another panic reaction to growing pressures is business' apparent hope that thousands more MBA graduates might make a difference. Somehow the MBA degree has supplanted the baccalaureate as a prerequisite to advancement. Yet the presence of more than a million MBA's has not made any appreciable difference in our productivity over the last decade. It could be argued, in fact, that the legions of graduates with the latest "union card" in their portfolio, have made the situation worse, not better. This is because their education has focused on quantitative analysis, financial manipulation and an irrelevant management framework.

Unfortunately, the MBA emphasis upon both money and the quantitative reinforces the ills of our society, meaning greed and abuse of power. Furthermore, the coveted degree is often earned on weekend or evening time while the student continues working. Thus, graduates are reinforced for workaholism, unbelievable stress management and denial of a personal, humanizing life. When, oh when, will we stop sacrificing the feminine values of feeling, meaning, relationship and play? Until people learn to balance themselves better internally, then balance their organizations too, we will be like the proverbial Mad Hatter—rushing to a future that makes no sense.

The Heart of the Crisis:
A New Concept of Self

While much of business (including government) continues to search in wrong directions for solutions to our growing crises, there is some evidence that a new era has arrived. In 1990 Peter Senge published *The Fifth Discipline: The Art and Practice of the Learning Organization,* and it is being widely read if not applied. Senge's book represents the most complete theoretical statement yet of the new management paradigm. As he suggests, at the heart of the learning organization is a "profound shift of mind." Senge furthermore points out that "personal mastery" is the first of the essential five disciplines needed to create this learning climate. His definition of personal mastery sounds amazingly like the portrait of the renewed, creative person described in Chapter Nine of this book. Senge is very sketchy, however, on *how* such personal mastery may be acquired.

My answer about the "how" is the growth sequence described in this book. Whether you experience the journey with the full-blown set of characteristics outlined, or whether your passage is of lesser intensity, self-definition and self-direction at deep levels is required. Thus, Senge's "personal mastery" is another term for the maturation process described in this book. The results include a changed mental outlook and changed behaviors as well. It involves recovering our dark side, going deep within and *un*learning much of what society and parents taught. It means becoming whole persons through a committed, long-term effort of plumbing personal depths. It means a radical but slow, cumulative shift of values and lifestyle. It means the decidedly hard, usually emotion-filled work of recovering feelings and vulnerability while also discovering essence.

One of the previously unspoken tenets about organizational renewal, or creating a true learning organization, is that it will require first and foremost a cadre of people who themselves have been transformed. Personal mastery *is* a prerequisite. The reason we need to start at the level of individual human change is simple. Those who have not been through a process of discovering their core self are unable to shed egocentric needs. They remain rooted in personal defenses which, in turn, means hanging onto fixed positions. Rigidity is the opposite of learning and change. Someone who needs to be "right," to stay in control is inflexible. The only type of person, however, who can flow with change, who can flip positions if need be, and who can share leadership is the person who understands surrender.

If we are to exist in organizations where there is constant learning and adaptation, then we must be able to see life itself as continual learning. The only type of person who can readily admit "mistakes" without losing face, is someone who has been humbled by the journey toward self. Out of such humility also comes compassion for life's lessons and foibles. The only type of person who can cope with rapid change without feeling threatened or losing one's center is the *open* person and system. Furthermore, the only type of person who can make ethical decisions *not* to produce shoddy products or to make things, such as violent movies, that potentially harm others, is someone who sees the relationship among things and accepts personal responsibility. And finally, those who have been through a deep process of self-discovery usually exhibit the desire to be involved with something larger than themselves. This desire to contribute is the opposite of the greed motive, which is a miscarriage of the organism's growth drive.

Toward a New Theory of Leadership

Forging a new concept of self through deep personal change would do much to produce leaders capable of creating learning organizations. For years Chris Argyris, Harvard professor and author, has been trying to teach executives the skills required for effective, open-ended communication. Such communication promotes what Argyris calls "double-loop learning," or the kind of learning that produces behavior change. He's found it an agonizingly slow process, mostly because managers have *un*conscious attitudes about being in control, not expressing feelings, being rational and winning (Argyris, 1982). Their beliefs get in the way of modifying their behavior, even when they say they want to speak and act differently.

Such attitudes, of course, are characteristic of the patriarchy and a masculine-oriented approach to life. These beliefs are typical, in other words, of the immature person, psychologically speaking, whether female or male, *before* they have gone through a transformative process. In contrast, undertaking deep personal change usually convinces us, quite consciously, that control can be readily yielded, that feelings are very important, that rationality is only one mode and that interactions aimed at winning are harmful. Despite the importance of Argyris' work, he too has missed the mark on *how* to bring about internal change. Arduous training as he suggests is not the solution; only deep personal development that plumbs the unconscious and brings about radical internal change can make the difference.

Over the last 20 years there has been much said and written about our "leadership crisis." The vacuum has prompted a reexamination of just what "the new leader" might need to be and do. Useful redefinition comes from such people as Senge, Harold Leavitt, Burt Nanus, Warren Bennis and John Greenleaf. Their identification of important leadership characteristics includes: foresight, insight and intuition, vision, sensitivity, personal purpose, mastery of change and interdependence, high ethics or integrity, excellent communication skills and the ability to use oneself. None of these experts, however, identifies *how* such qualities can be developed.

Again, the answer is that the inner journey is the route. When one compares the outcomes of personal transformation with the qualities needed by "the new leader" there is a stunning correlation. Deep personal change, where we come to terms with ourselves at new levels, is what gives us the capacity and strength for leadership. As one young middle manager suggested about his promotion, "It is only *because* my wife went through a treatment center and triggered my stay there too (for co-dependency), plus all the subsequent therapy and personal work, that I am able to assume a leadership position. The more inner work I've done, the more confident I am that I can lead and help others develop their full potential."

The man's statement illustrates the point: Leadership is *not* about a set of teachable skills that can be ingested in a classroom by manipulating facts, numbers or theories. Neither is it a list of seven habits or 12 characteristics that can be memorized, copied or willed into place. Such portraits can only provide a vision about growth. True leadership, however, is an inner development process that can only be encouraged or mentored. It is about the honing of character. Finally we know much more about what character involves. Such understanding can be incorporated into innovative mentoring/coaching approaches. We need to remember, however, that leadership unfolds in its own time, only when the person is ready. The process cannot be pushed or forced. The end result is self-knowledge and the conviction to lead.

The idea that self-awareness is the most important criteria for leadership has interesting implications. Carried to its logical conclusion, it means that *anyone* can be a leader, whether placed in a formal position to do so or not. The ability to empower many to assume leadership roles is more evident in knowledge industries. In these companies the nature of the task constantly changes. Work is complex, interrelated and fast-paced. People simply have to rely upon one another; they cannot wait for direction from a formal leader.

As Will Schutz, human potential guru turned organization consultant, suggested in a 1991 workshop on "Organization Renewal in the '90s", true self-awareness means that you can then play to your own strengths and fully utilize those of others. The visionary, for example, can employ that skill while leaning on others for technical leadership. Conversely, the technical person can provide their expertise, knowing that visionary strength must come from someone else. Similarly, the person who quietly goes about putting things together in a collaborative mode can be every bit the leader too. Many of our expectations, that a leader "take charge" or be out in front, are due for overhaul. Instead, self-knowledge and knowing how to use the self are key.

The task of leadership development becomes further simplified when we add the other basics to what a leader really needs to know. These basics, says Schutz, include "1) knowing what the task involves, or the job at hand, 2) knowing the strengths of others, and 3) understanding something about how groups work." Armed with these basics, plus a solid sense of self, some amazing results, not to mention spontaneity and fun, can be produced. The complexity in the process is that self-awareness takes time and hard, inner work. Self-knowledge and openness also must be multiplied throughout the team.

An Unclaimed Revolution:
A Vision to Nurture

A new concept of self and the healing to bring that about is needed in circles far beyond leadership development. In fact, almost any current crisis can be related to the need for higher consciousness. That is, if we had many more engaged in deep personal change, numerous problems might be solved or transcended. Child and domestic abuse, for example, emerges from *un*conscious parents or partners who themselves have been abused. Widespread inner healing could change this. In addition, psychological damage that can be traced to low quality child rearing shows up in a multitude of other social problems, from mental health facilities to welfare rolls. Prison populations grow and crime increases because we haven't solved other crises, such as drugs and poverty; our rehabilitation programs are pitifully inadequate. Healing troubled souls seems far from our minds and hearts. In the world at large, the environment and economy are in danger because unethical, shortsighted decisions have been made without concern for the larger good. Our political leadership lacks vision and direction because self-knowledge has never been valued. Instead, outer performance and how we look are all-important. George Bush is one of the best examples of a man who did all "the right things" to become President but never defined his character.

On and on the list could go. The point is that lack of higher human consciousness is at the root of most of the world's ills. What then, might be the prospects for widespread healing and change? What is business' potential contribution?

The signals at the moment appear mixed. Some disturbing, countervailing trends exist. On the dark side is a seeming endorsement from public figures that subterfuge and denial are acceptable. Racism and intolerance are pervasive and subtly entrenched. Widespread malaise persists. High debt levels, corruption, abuse of power, still-rampant materialism and leadership paralysis plague us.

The news stories, however, usually don't cover the most hopeful signs. One of the most striking is that thousands in this country have already been through deep personal change; many more attend support and healing groups of every kind. Many who have done the inner work have entered through the wounds of addiction and recovery. Indeed, there was a 1989 joke that you'd better hurry up and claim an addiction soon; otherwise you'd be left out in the '90s. The recovery movement has been sweeping across America like a prairie fire for at least five years. In November 1991, John Bradshaw, the counselor, workshop guru and author of best-selling *Homecoming,* made the middle pages of *Time* magazine. For several years now Bradshaw has been packing crowds into workshops on "healing the inner child."

Another encouraging note is that some local communities no longer wait for Washington to solve problems; they have seized the initiative and are mobilizing effective grass roots coalitions. Even the network news shows highlight success stories and model projects. Some women are angry enough about the abortion issue to become more serious about politics; more men are finding their way to a men's movement that helps heal patriarchal wounds.

Another positive, invisible phenomenon is a growing web of formal and informal networks crisscrossing the nation and beyond. Such networks link people with similar professional interests or merely provide personal support; increasingly they are becoming computerized. Eventually this linkage could electrify the world. Finally, there are "new paradigm" centers sprouting everywhere to educate people about transformative options. Their expertise ranges from organic farming to solar living, various forms of therapy, self-publishing and resource-sharing. Most are currently only fledgling operations; they are seeds, however, of new ways to live on this planet.

All of these near-invisible signs of rebirth represent enormous people-power. Although they've barely been noticed publicly, their presence suggests that a human potential revolution has been unleashed without being fully claimed. The word, "revolution," means radical change, or the throwing off of one form for another. Those who have undertaken deep personal change go through just such a radical adjustment within themselves. Many did that in the '80s, and now we are seeing the first fruits of their willingness to act after inner retreat.

Why has such a profound development gone unnoticed in the media? Partly because the change occurs gradually, internally, over a long period. Those who have experienced deep personal change are also just now reaching influential positions. In addition, our "naming" of this movement has been problem-oriented rather than positive. Thus, we've missed the explosive healing potential. To admit addictions, for example, implies "problems." Many people can't or don't want to identify with that. Yet society itself is addiction-based, and those with "the problems" are leading the way to higher mental health. Until recently we have not understood that deep psychic readjustment is required for human maturation. Those most wounded by a patriarchal society, however, have been forced to insights. Thus, the good news is that a large number of people, from every walk of life, has already experienced the process of deep personal change. They are ready now to be teachers, mentors, guides, therapists and friends to countless others.

Many who have been through deep personal change cannot describe their turmoil-filled experience. They know, however, that there is "life after death." Renewal is possible. One of the most exciting things about this new vision of human nature is that the applications will be unending. First is the spector of what might happen when thousands more are released to their unique purpose and potential. The flowering could be awesome. But broader applications are also possible. Once we understand the transformative process itself, we can use it everywhere.

Transformation, for example, or deep personal change, is synonymous with deep learning, or the double-loop learning of Gregory Bateson, Chris Argyris and Peter Senge. Such understanding could revolutionize education. But the knowledge base promises more than that. With a bit more work from a synthesis task force, for example, we could understand far more fully how teams and organizations learn. This would give us the HOW of dealing with change at individual, group and larger system levels. Such a body of knowledge, a desperately needed "technology of transformation," could be applied extensively. Organizations the world over are in need of knowing how to develop and reform. Many of our problems, in fact, are not affected by scarce resources so much as by wasted or ill-used ones. Consolidating the new management paradigm could make a significant contribution to effective resource utilization.

Finally, the understanding of the transformative process itself is synonymous with healing and creativity. People who go through the stages described in this book become whole people. Imagine what might happen to the physically ill, the mentally ill and the criminal if long-term, in-depth psychological treatment was available? Yes, there are probably limitations to the success stories. Yet so many could be helped to become more whole if we but believed that human beings possessed a loving core at the center. Such healing would require extensive treatment resources, yet the money now used for warehousing, maintenance or dealing with repeat offenders solves little.

But what does all of this have to do with business? If society is going to be transformed, then the business sector's healing of itself is in order. In centuries past the church or the state was capable of initiating widespread cultural change. Today, however, we live in a society where business capital is the deciding factor. Real power and influence lies in the economic sector.

There are some preliminary signs that business will be in the vanguard. Already many are interested in books about "meaning and fulfillment," creativity and intuition. Business people are also feeling the pinch of personal change. Panic and trauma, the kind that pushes us inward, is affecting many who are most likely to have the resources to pursue personal growth.

Ironically, the more precarious our economy, the more our institutions are in turmoil, the greater chance that individuals will be forced to their inner work. Forcing America to its knees, in other words, is healthy. True humility has nothing to do with weakness and everything to do with becoming fully human.

The importance of involving the business tier of society in deep personal change and renewal cannot be underestimated. This is because the business segment controls so much that affects our future, from pollution decisions to car safety, energy needs and how we die and care for people. No other segment of our population, including government, religion, education or medicine, has the potential to do so much good. Patriarchal excesses have created conditions demanding fundamental change, but a new era may be at hand.

Despite our current malaise, in fact, the business sector is far more open than others to rebirth. Pragmatism, realism, and an orientation to bottom-line results characterize business. Our long history of adaptation and entrepreneurship means that American business *can* make a comeback of significant proportions. Only in America has there been the freedom of opportunity to pursue one's dreams, free of the constraints of class or ethnic origin. That extreme emphasis on the individual has run amok in recent years, producing egocentric greed and power abuse. At the next stage, however, through deep personal change, comes rebirth and renewal. We must nurture the vision of this possible dream.

Epilogue:
An Invitation to Readers

In order to further test the conclusions found in this book, readers are invited to share their subjective experiences as part of a research project. The impetus for such an invitation comes from Ken Wilber's ideas about subjecting contemplative/spiritual knowledge to the test of *communality*.

Wilber's important insight about *knowing* is that there are at least three modes—sensory, symbolic and contemplative. Only the sensory mode is subject to empirical or scientific verification; the symbolic is subject to interpretation, and the contemplative can be understood only if you have developed "the eye" to see it. Credibility in the symbolic and contemplative areas is established by whether or not interpretations and insights are shared by others.

Wilber sets out his thesis in two important first chapters of *Eye to Eye* (1983). Indeed, if these pages were understood in graduate schools and research institutions, we would probably see drastic changes in much of the behavioral and physical science "research" being conducted. Whole disciplines might reorganize and redefine themselves; some careers could be deeply affected.

Other sources that substantiate different types of knowing include Deikman's chapter, "Mysticism as A Science," in *The Observing Self* (1982) and Harman and Rheingold's treatment, "The Still Small Voice: Toward a New Science of Religion" in *Higher Creativity* (1984). In addition, Abraham Maslow believed that our inner nature could be objectively, scientifically studied through inner search and psychotherapy; Fritjof Capra suggests that the new science of consciousness is a process of model-making based on inner experience (*The Turning Point,* 1982). Morris Berman, in *The Reenchantment of the World* (1984), creates the case that conscious, empirical knowledge contains a fundamental error in our understanding of human nature; continued reliance on it now threatens our survival. Stanislav Grof's view of the changing paradigm in *Beyond The Brain* (1985), shows how the behavioral sciences were affected by early science without updating themselves as a result of the discoveries of quantum physics.

All of these thinkers challenge the premises of science itself. Certainly science has a place, but the argument that information now labeled as "metaphysical," "mystic" or "paranormal" is invalid falls apart in the face of an expanded framework. Nonetheless, many today still cling to notions about "proof" and "objective observation" because they haven't examined the assumptions behind the scientific paradigm. What others are saying, however, is that such knowledge *can* be verified; it is just that we must test it in a different way. Hence comes my interest in hearing from ordinary people about their personal/spiritual growth, and whether and how the ideas set forth in this book might be modified. Such an invitation also demonstrates what it means to be "an open system."

Readers interested in sharing their personal experiences are encouraged to respond to the following questions in five typed pages or less. (Legible handwriting is acceptable if typing is prohibitive.)

A. Attach a blank cover page with the following:
Name:_____
Address:_____
Phone:_____(home)_____(work)
Date of Birth:_____
Follow-up inquiries (phone, mail or interview), if initiated by the author or her staff, are OK: _____Yes_____No.

B. Please respond to the following:
1. Do the stages of growth as described in this book confirm your experience? If so, what refinements or elaborations would you add?
2. If the stages do *not* fit your experience, what variances can you describe?
3. What therapeutic methods, spiritual practices or informal growth tools were important in your experience?
4. How long did this process take to unfold?
5. Can you substantiate your experiences through journal notes or second-person reports from a therapist or guide?
6. Additional comments, if any.

All information will be treated confidentially. Participants, should understand, however, that responses will be potentially publishable in the form of anonymous quotes or disguised descriptions. Responses should be mailed to:

> INNER Research
> c/o Alice Mack, Ed.D.
> 7344 North Oracle Road, Suite 194
> Tucson, AZ 85704

Please mark the envelope "Personal and Confidential".

Synthesis Comparsions

Structure of the Psyche

Lowen _Bioenergetics_	Deikman _The Observing Self_	Wilber _No Boundry_	Grof _Beyond the Brain_	Common to Many
Ego Defense	Thinking Self	Ego Level	Sensory Barrier	Intellectual
Muscle Defense	Functional Self	Centaur	Psychodynamic	Physical
Emotional Defense	Emotional Self	Transpersonal	Perinatal	Emotional
Core	Observing Self	Transpersonal Mind	Transpersonal	Spirtual

Table I. Structure of the Psyche

This table shows how various contemporary thinkers have described the four levels of the psyche that must be penetrated in order to attain growth at higher levels. Jung's understanding was similar. He described layers that included 1) Ego consciousness, 2) the personal unconscious, 3) the collective unconscious, or transpersonal, and 4) the psychoid level. (From _Jung, Synchronicity and Human Destiny_ by Progoff.) For purposes of simplicity and synthesis, this book has chosen to name these as the intellectual, physical, emotional and spiritual levels.

Stages, or the Process of Growth

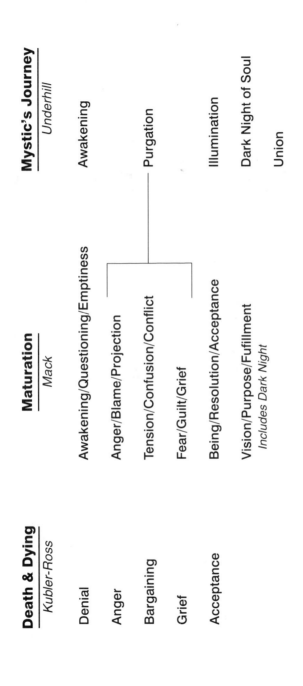

Death & Dying	Maturation	Mystic's Journey
Kubler-Ross	*Mack*	*Underhill*
Denial	Awakening/Questioning/Emptiness	Awakening
Anger	Anger/Blame/Projection	Purgation
Bargaining	Tension/Confusion/Conflict	
Grief	Fear/Guilt/Grief	
Acceptance	Being/Resolution/Acceptance	Illumination
	Vision/Purpose/Fufillment	Dark Night of Soul
	Includes Dark Night	Union

Table II. Stages, or the Process of Inner Growth and Maturation

This table compares Elisabeth Kubler-Ross' naming of the death and dying experience and Evelyn Underhill's understanding of the mystic journey to the author's descriptive words for each stage.

References

Anonymous, *A Course In Miracles*. Foundation for Inner Peace: Tiburon, CA, 1975.

Allen, Paula Gunn, *The Sacred Hoop: Recovering the Feminine in American Indian Traditions*. Boston: Beacon Press, 1986.

Almaas, A.H., Essence: The Diamond Approach to Inner Realization. York Beach, Maine: Samuel Weiser, Inc., 1986.

————, *The Void: A Psychodynamic Investigation of the Relationship Between Mind and Space*. Berkeley: Diamond Books-Almaas Publications, 1986.

Andrews, Lewis M., *To Thine Own Self Be True: The Relationship Between Spiritual Values and Emotional Health*. New York: Doubleday, 1987, 1989.

Anthony, Dick, Ecker, Bruce and Wilber, Ken, eds., *Spiritual Choices: The Problems of Recognizing Authentic Paths to Inner Transformation*. New York: Paragon House Publishers, 1987.

Argyris, Chris. "The Executive Mind and Double-Loop Learning. *Organizational Dynamics*. New York: Autumn, 1982.

Argyris, Chris and Schon, Donald A., *Theory In Practice: Increasing Professional Effectiveness*. San Francisco: Jossey-Bass Publishers, 1974.

Belenky, Mary Field, Clinchy, Blythe McVicker, Goldberger, Nancy Rule and Tarule, Jill Mattuck. *Women's Ways of Knowing: The Development of Self, Voice and Mind*. New York: Basic Books, Inc., 1986.

Bennet, E. A., *What Jung Really Said*. New York: Schoken Books, 1966.

Bennis, Warren. *Why Leaders Can't Lead: The Unconscious Conspiracy Continues*. San Francisco: Jossey-Bass Publishers, 1989.

————, *On Becoming A Leader*. Reading, Massachusetts: Addison-Wesley Publishing Co., 1989.

————, and Nanus, Burt. *Leaders: The Strategies for Taking Charge*. New York: Harper & Row, 1985.

Bentov, Itzhak, *Stalking the Wild Pendulum: On the Mechanics of Consciousness*. New York: Bantam, 1977.

Berman, Morris, *The Reenchantment of the World*. New York: Bantam, 1984.

———, *Coming to Our Senses: Body and Spirit in the Hidden History of the West*. New York: Bantam, 1989.

Bly, Robert. *Iron John: A Book About Men*. Reading, Massachusetts: Addison-Wesley Publishing Co., 1990.

Borysenko, Joan. *Guilt is the Teacher: Love is the Lesson*. New York: Warner Books, Inc. 1990.

Boyd, Doug, *Rolling Thunder*. New York: Delta, 1974.

Bradshaw, John, *Bradshaw On: The Family: A revolutionary Way of Self-Discovery*. Pompano Beach, Florida: Health Communications, Inc., 1988.

———, *Healing the Shame That Binds You*. Deerfield Beach, Florida: Health Communications, Inc., 1988.

Bragdon, Emma. *The Call of Spiritual Emergency: From Personal Crisis to Personal Transformation*. San Francisco: Harper & Row, 1990.

Bridges, William, *Transitions: Making Sense of Life's Changes*. Reading, Massachusetts: Addison-Wesley Publishing Co., 1980.

Bucke, Richard Maurice, *Cosmic Consciousness*. New York: E.P. Dutton, 1969.

Campbell, Joseph, *Myths To Live By*. New York: Bantam, 1972.

———, with Bill Moyers, *The Power of Myth*. New York: Doubleday, 1988.

———, *The Hero with a Thousand Faces*. Princeton: Princeton University Press, 2nd edition, 1968.

———, in conversation with Michael Toms, *An Open Life*. Burdett, New York: Larson Publications, 1988.

Capra, Fritjof. *The Turning Point*. New York: Bantam Books, 1985.

———, *Uncommon Wisdom: Conversations with Remarkable People*. New York: Bantam, 1989.

Carey, K.X., *The Starseed Transmissions: An Extraterrestrial Report. Raphael*. Kansas City: Uni-Sun, 1982.

————, *Terra Christa: The Global Spiritual Awakening*. Kansas City: Uni-Sun, 1985.

Christ, Carol P., *Diving Deep and Surfacing: Woman Writers on Spiritual Quest*. Boston: Beacon Press, 1980.

————, and Plaskow, Judith, eds., *Womanspirit Rising: A Feminist Reader in Religion*. San Francisco: Harper & Row, 1979.

Collin, Rodney, *The Theory of Conscious Harmony*. Boulder & London: Shambhala, 1984.

Teilhard De Chardin, Pierre, *The Phenonmenon of Man*. New York: Harper & Row, 1959.

Deikman, Arthur J., *The Observing Self: Mysticism and Psychotherapy*. Boston: Beacon Press, 1982.

DesRoches, Brian. *Re-claiming Your Self: The Co-dependent's Recovery Plan*. New York: Dell Trade Paperback, 1990.

Dobyns, Lloyd and Crawford-Mason, Clare. *Quality or Else*. Boston: Houghton Mifflin, 1991.

Dossey, Larry, *Beyond Illness: Discovering the Experience of Health*. Boulder & London: Shambhala, New Science Library, 1984.

Eisler, Riane, *The Chalice and The Blade: Our History, Our Future*. San Francisco: Harper & Row, 1987.

Enomiya-Lassale, Hugo, *Living in the New Consciousness*. Boston & Shaftesbury: Shambhala, 1988.

Ferguson, Marilyn, *The Aquarian Conspiracy: Personal and Social Transformation in the 1980's*. Los Angeles: J.P. Tarcher, Inc., 1980.

Ferrucci, Piero, *What We May Be: Techniques for Psychological and Spiritual Growth Through Psychosynthesis*. Los Angeles: Jeremy P. Tarcher, Inc., 1982.

————, *Inevitable Grace: Breakthroughs in the Lives of Great Men and Women: Guides to Your Self-Realization*. Los Angeles: Jeremy P. Tarcher, Inc. 1990.

Fox, Matthew. *Original Blessing*. Santa Fe: Bear & Co., 1983.

————, *The Coming of the Cosmic Christ: The Healing of Mother Earth and the Birth of A Global Renaissance*. San Francisco: Harper & Row, 1988.

French, Marilyn, *Beyond Power: On Women, Men and Morals*. New York: Ballantine Books, 1985.

Fromm, Erich, *For The Love Of Life*. Translated from the German by Robert and Rita Kimber; ed., Hans Jurgen Schultz. New York: The Free Press, 1986.

Fritz, Robert, *The Path of Least Resistance: Principles for Creating What You Want to Create*. Salem, Massachusetts: DMA, Inc., 1984.

Gilligan, Carol, *In A Difference Voice*. Cambridge: Harvard University Press, 1982.

Goldberg, Philip. *The Intuitive Edge*. Los Angeles: Jeremy P. Tarcher, Inc., 1983.

Gould, Roger L., *Transformations: Growth and Change in Adult Life*. New York: Simon & Schuster, 1978.

Greenleaf, Robert K. *Servant Leadership*. New York: Paulist Press, 1977, 1991.

Griscom, Chris, *Ectasy Is A New Frequency*. Santa Fe: Bear & Co., 1987.

Grof, Stanislav, *Realms of the Human Unconscious: Observations from LSD Research*. New York: E.P. Dutton, 1976.

————, *Beyond the Brain: Birth, Death and Transcendence in Psychotherapy*. Albany: State University of New York Press, 1985.

————, *The Adventure of Self-Discovery*. Albany: State University of New York Press, 1988.

————, and Christina, Eds. *Spiritual Emergency: When Personal Transformation Becomes A Crisis*. Los Angeles: Jeremy P. Tarcher, 1989.

————, and Christina. *The Stormy Search for the Self: A Guide to Personal Growth through Transformational Crisis*. Los Angeles: Jeremy P. Tarcher, Inc. 1990.

Handy, Charles. *The Age of Unreason*. Boston: Harvard Business School Press, 1989.

Halifax, Joan, *Shamanic Voices*. New York: E.P. Dutton, 1979.

Harding, Esther. *Psychic Energy: Its Source and Its Transformation*. 2nd Edition. Princeton: Princeton University Press, 1963.

Harding, Esther M., *Woman's Mysteries: Ancient and Modern*. New York: Harper Colophon, 1971.

Harman, Willis, *Global Mind Change: The Promise of the Last Years of the Twentieth Century*. Indianapolis: Knowledge Systems, Inc., 1988.

————, and Rheingold, Howard, *Higher Creativity: Liberating the Unconscious for Breakthrough Insights*. Los Angeles: Jeremy P. Tarcher, Inc., 1984

————, and Hormann, John. *Creative Work: The Constructive Role of Business in a Transforming Society*. Indianapolis: Knowledge Systems, Inc., 1990.

Harner, Michael, *The Way of the Shaman: Guide to Power and Healing*. New York: Bantam Books, 1980.

Heckler, Richard. *The Anatomy of Change: East/West Approaches to Body/Mind Therapy*. Boulder & London: Shambhala, 1984.

Hendricks, Gay, and Fadiman, James, eds., *Transpersonal Education: A Curriculum for Feeling and Being*. Englewood Cliffs: Prentice-Hall, Inc., 1976.

Hickman, Craig and Silva, Michael. *Creating Excellence*. New York: New American Library, 1984.

Highwater, Jamake, *The Primal Mind: Vision and Reality in Indian America*. New York: New American Library, 1981.

Hinz, Evelyn J., ed., *Anais Nin: A Woman Speaks*. Chicago: The Swallow Press, 1975.

Jaccobi, Jolande, *The Way of Individuation*. New York: New American Library, 1965.

————, *The Psychology of C.G. Jung*. New Haven & London: Yale University Press, 1973.

Jampolsky, Gerald G. *Out of Darkness Into the Light: A Journey of Inner Healing*. New York: Bantam, 1989.

Johnson, Robert, *He: Understanding Masculine Psychology*. New York: Perennial Library, 1974.

—————, *She: Understanding Feminine Psychology*. New York: Perennial Library, 1976.

—————, *We: Understanding the Psychology of Romantic Love*. San Francisco: Harper & Row: 1983.

—————, *Femininity Lost and Regained*. New York: Harper & Row, 1990.

Johnston, Charles M., *The Creative Imperative*. Berkeley: Celestial Arts, 1984/1986.

Jones, Landon Y., *Great Expectations: America and the Baby Boom Generation*. New York: Ballantine Books, 1980.

Joy, W. Brugh, *Joy's Way: A Map for the Transformational Journey*. Los Angeles: J.P. Tarcher Inc., 1979.

—————, *Avalanche: Heretical Reflections on the Dark and the Light*. New York: Ballantine Books, 1990.

Jung, Carl, translated by R.F.C. Hull, *The Portable Jung*. New York: Penguin Books, 1971.

Kavanaugh, Kieron and Rodriguez, Otilio, trans., *The Collected Works of St. John of the Cross*. Washington: Institute of Carmelite Studies, 1979.

Keen, Sam. *Fire In the Belly*. New York: Bantam Books, 1991.

Khan, Hazrat Inayat, *Spiritual Dimensions of Psychology*. Lebanon Springs, New York: Sufi Order Publications, 1981.

Kiefer, Gene, Ed., *Kundalini for the New Age: Selected Writings by Gopi Krishna*. New York: Bantam Books, 1988.

Kopp, Sheldon, *If You Meet the Buddha on the Road, Kill Him!* New York: Bantam Books, 1972.

Kotter, John P. *The Leadership Factor*. New York: The Free Press, 1988.

Kubler-Ross, Elisabeth, *On Death and Dying*. New York: Macmillan Publishing Co., Inc., 1969.

————, *Questions and Answers on Death and Dying*. New York: Macmillan Publishing Co., Inc., 1974.

————, *Death: The Final Stage of Growth*. Englewood Cliffs: Prentice-Hall, Inc., 1975.

————, *To Live Until We Say Goodbye*. Englewood Cliffs: Prentice-Hall, Inc., 1978.

————, *Living with Death and Dying*. New York: Macmillan Publishing Co., 1981.

————, and Warshaw, Mal, *Working It Through*. New York: Macmillan Publishing Co., Inc., 1982.

————, *On Children and Death*. New York: Macmillan Publishing Co., 1983.

Kuhn, Thomas S., *The Structure of Scientific Revolutions. 2nd Edition,* Chicago: University of Chicago Press, 1970.

LaBier, Douglas, *Modern Madness: The Emotional Fallout of Success.* Reading, Massachusetts.: Addison-Wesley Publishing Co., Inc. 1986.

Laing, R.D., *The Politics of Experience*. New York: Ballantine Books, 1967,

————, *The Divided Self.* New York: Penguin Books, 1969.

Lame Deer, John and Erdoes, Richard, *Lame Deer: Seeker of Visions*. New York: Washington Square Press Pocket Books, 1972.

Land, George T., *Grow or Die: The Unifying Principle of Transformation.* New York: John Wiley & Sons, (reissued edition), 1986.

Leavitt, Harold J., *Corporate Pathfinders*. New York: Penguin Books, 1986.

————, "Educating Our MBAs: On Teaching What We Haven't Taught." *California Management Review*. Berkeley: University of California, Spring, 1989.

Lee, John H., *The Flying Boy: Healing the Wounded Man*. Deerfield Beach, Florida: Health Communications, Inc., 1987.

Lenz, Elinor and Myerhoff, Barbara, *The Feminization of America*. Los Angeles: Jeremy P. Tarcher, 1985.

Leonard, George B., *The Transformation: A Guide to the Inevitable Changes in Humankind.* Los Angeles: J.P. Tarcher, Inc., 1972.

Leonard, Linda S., *The Wounded Woman: Healing the Father-Daughter Relationship.* Boulder & London: Shambhala, 1983.

Levine, Stephen, *Who Dies? An Investigation of Conscious Living and Conscious Dying.* New York: Anchor Press/Doubleday, 1982.

Lowen, Alexander, *Bioenergetics.* New York: Penguin Books, 1975.

Luthman, Shirley Gehrke, *Intimacy: The Essence of Male and Female.* San Rafael, California: Mehetabel & Co., 1972.

————, *Collection 1979.* San Rafael, California: Mehetabel & Co., 1980.

————, *Energy and Personal Power.* San Rafael, California: Mehetabel & Co., 1982.

MacLaine, Shirley, *Out On A Limb.* New York: Bantam Books, 1983.

————, *Dancing in the Light.* New York: Bantam Books, 1985.

Marrs, Donald. *Executive in Passage.* Los Angeles: Barrington Sky Publishing, 1990.

Maslow, Abraham H., *Motivation and Personality, 2nd Edition,* New York: Harper & Row, 1954.

————, *Toward A Psychology of Being, 2nd Edition,* New York: D. Van Nostrand Co., 1968.

————, *The Farther Reaches of Human Nature.* New York: The Viking Press, 1971.

McDermott, Robert A. *The Essential Aurobindo.* Great Barrington, Massachusetts: Lindisfarne Press, 1987.

Mead, Margaret, *Culture and Commitment: A Study of the Generation Gap.* Garden City, New York: Natural History Press/Doubleday & Co., 1970.

Miller, Alice, *The Drama of the Gifted Child.* New York: Basic Books, 1981.

————, *For Your Own Good: Hidden Cruelty in Child-Rearing and the Roots of Violence.* New York: Farrar, Straus, Giroux, 1983, 1984.

————, *Thou Shalt Not Be Aware: Society's Betrayal of the Child.* New York: Farrar, Straus, Giroux, 1984.

————, *Breaking Down the Wall of Silence.* New York: Dutton, 1991.

Miller, Jean Baker, *Toward A New Psychology of Women.* Boston: Beacon Press, 1976.

Montagu, Ashley, *The Natural Superiority of Women.* New York: Collier Books Revised Edition, 1968.

Moss, Richard, *The I That Is We.* Berkeley: Celestial Arts, 1981.

————, *The Black Butterfly: An Invitation to Radical Aliveness.* Berkeley: Celestial Arts, 1986.

Nanus, Burt. *The Leader's Edge.* Chicago: Contemporary Books, 1989.

Niehardt, John C., *Black Elk Speaks.* New York: Washington Square Press Pocket Books, 1959.

Neumann, Erich, *Amor and Psyche: The Psychic Development of the Feminine.* Princeton: Princeton University Press, 1956.

————, *The Origins and History of Consciousness.* Princeton: Princeton University Press, 1970.

————, *Depth Psychology and A New Ethic.* Boston and Shaftesbury: Shambhala, 1990.

Nicoll, Maurice. *The New Man.* Boulder & London: Shambhala, 1984.

Nichols, Michael P., *Turning Forty in the '80s: Personal Crisis, Time for Change.* New York: W.W. Norton & Co., 1986.

Nouwen, Henri J.M., *The Wounded Healer: Ministry in Contemporary Society.* Garden City, New York: Image Books, 1979.

Peck, M. Scott, *The Road Less Traveled: A New Psychology of Love, Traditional Values and Spiritual Growth.* New York: Simon & Schuster, 1978.

————, *The Different Drum: Community-Making and Peace*. New York: Simon & Schuster, 1987.

Pelletier, Kenneth R., *Toward A Science of Consciousness*. Berkeley: Celestial Arts, 1985.

Peters, Thomas and Waterman, Robert H. *In Search of Excellence: Lessons from America's Best-Run Companies*. New York: Harper & Row, 1982.

————, *Thriving on Chaos: Handbook for a Management Revolution*. New York: Harper & Row, 1987.

Petersen-Lowary, Sheila, *The 5th Dimension: Channels to A New Reality*. New York: Simon & Schuster, Inc., 1988.

Progoff, Ira, *The Death and Rebirth of Psychology*. New York: McGraw Hill, 1956.

————, *Jung's Psychology and Its Social Meaning*. Garden City, New York: Anchor Press/Doubleday, 1973.

————, *Jung, Synchronicity and Human Destiny: C.G. Jung's Theory of Meaningful Coincidence*. New York: Julian Press, 1973.

Reid, Clyde M., *Dreams: Discovering Your Inner Teacher*. Minneapolis: Winston Press, Inc., 1983.

Rich, Adrienne, *Of Woman Born: Motherhood As Experience and Institution*. New York: W.W. Norton & Co., 1976.

Roberts, Bernadette, *The Experience of No-Self*. Boulder: Shambhala, 1984.

Rudhyar, Dane, *Occult Preparations for A New Age*. Wheaton, Illinois: Theosophical Publishing House, 1975.

————, *Culture, Crisis and Creativity*. Wheaton, Illinois: Theosophical Publishing House, 1977.

————, *Beyond Individualism: The Psychology of Transformation*. Wheaton, Illinois: Theosophical Publishing House, 1979.

Russel, Peter, *The Global Brain*. Los Angeles: J.P. Tarcher, Inc., 1983.

Sanford, John, *The Kingdon Within: A Study of the Inner Meaning of Jesus's Sayings*. New York/Ramsey: Paulist Press, 1970.

————, *Healing and Wholeness*. New York: Paulist Press, 1977.

————, *Invisible Partners: How the Male and Female In Each of Us Affects Our Relationships*. New York: Paulist Press, 1980.

————, ed. and commentator, *Fritz Kunkel: Selected Writings*. New York: Paulist Press, 1984.

Sargent, Alice G., *The Androgynous Manager*. New York: Amacom, 1981.

Satprem. *Sri Aurobindo or the Adventure of Consciousness*. New York: Institute for Evolutionary Research, 1984.

Schaef, Anne Wilson. *Women's Reality: An Emerging Female System in the White Male Society*. Minneapolis: Winston Press, 1981.

————, *Co-Dependence: Misunderstood-Mistreated*. San Francisco: Harper & Row, 1986.

————, *When Society Becomes An Addict*. San Francisco: Harper & Row, 1987.

————, and Fassel, Diane. *The Addictive Organization*. San Francisco: Harper & Row, 1988.

Senge, Peter. *The Fifth Discipline: The Art and Practice of the Learning Organization*. New York: Doubleday Currency, 1990.

Sheehy, Gail, *Passages: Predictable Crises of Adult Life*. New York: E. P. Dutton & Co., Inc., 1974, 1976.

————, *Character: America's Search For Leadership*. New York: William Morrow & Co., Inc., 1988.

Siegel, Bernie S. *Peace, Love and Healing*. New York: Harper & Row, 1989.

Singer, June, *Boundaries of the Soul*. Garden City, New York: Anchor Books, 1973.

————, *Seeing Through the Visible World*. San Francisco: Harper Collins, 1991.

Small, Jacquelyn, *Transformers: The Therapists of the Future*. Marina del Rey, California: De Vorss & Co., 1982.

Spretnak, Charlene, ed., *The Politics of Women's Spirituality*. Garden City, New York: Anchor Books, 1982.

Stein, Murray, ed., *Jungian Analysis*. Boulder & London: Shambhala, 1984.

————, *In Mid-Life: A Jungian Perspective*. Dallas: Spring Publications, Inc. 1983.

————, *Jung's Treatment of Christianity*. Wilmette, Illinois, Chiron Publications, 1986.

Steiner, Rudolph, *Knowledge of the Higher Worlds and Its Attainment*. Spring Valley, New York: Anthroposophic Press, 1947.

Storm, Hyemeyohsts, *Seven Arrows*. New York: Ballantine Books, 1972.

Sun Bear, as told to Wabun and Barry Weinstock, *The Path of Power*. Spokane: Bear Tribe Publishing, 1983.

Trevelyan, George, *Summons To A High Crusade*. The Park, "Forres IV36 OTZ", Scotland: The Findhorn Press, 1986.

————, *A Vision of the Aquarian Age*. Walpole, New Hampshire: Stillpoint Publishing, 1984.

Ulanov, Ann Belford, *The Feminine in Jungian Psychology and In Christian Theology*. Evanston, Illinois: Northwestern University Press, 1971.

————, *Receiving Woman: Studies in the Psychology and Theology of the Feminine*. Philadelphia: The Westminster Press, 1981.

Underhill, Evelyn, *Mysticism: A Study in the Nature and Development of Man's Spiritual Consciousness*. New York: New American Library, 1974.

Vaughn, Frances E., *Awakening Intuition*. Garden City, New York: Anchor Press/Doubleday, 1979.

————, *The Inward Arc: Healing and Wholeness in Psychotherapy and Spirituality*. Boston & London: Shambhala, New Science Library, 1986.

Walker, Alice, *The Color Purple*. New York: Pocket Books, 1982.

Walsh, Roger, *Staying Alive: The Psychology of Human Survival*. Boulder & London: New Science Library, Shambhala, 1984.

————, and Vaughn, Frances, eds., *Beyond Ego: Transpersonal Dimensions in Psychology*. Los Angeles: J.P. Tarcher, Inc., 1980.

Washburn, Michael, *The Ego and the Dynamic Ground: A Transpersonal Theory of Human Development*. Albany: State University of New York Press, 1988.

Waterman, Robert H., *The Renewal Factor: How the Best Get and Keep the Competitive Edge*. New York: Bantam Books, 1987.

Waters, Frank, *Book of the Hopi*. New York: Penguin Books, 1984.

Watts, Alan W., *Psychotherapy East and West*. New York: New American Library, 1961.

Wegscheider-Cruse, Sharon. *The Miracle of Recovery*. Deerfield Beach, Florida: Health Communications, Inc. 1989.

Welwood, John, *Awakening the Heart: East/West Approaches to Psychotherapy and the Healing Relationship*. Boulder & London: Shambhala, 1983.

————, Ed. *Challenge of the Heart: Love, Sex and Intimacy in Changing Times*. Boston: Shambhala, 1985.

White, John, ed., *What Is Enlightenment: Exploring the Goal of the Spiritual Path*. Los Angeles: Jeremy P. Tarcher, Inc., 1984.

Whitmont, Edward C., *The Return of the Goddess*. New York: Crossroad, 1984.

Wickes, Frances G., *The Inner World of Choice*. Englewood Cliffs: Prentice-Hall, Inc., 1976.

Wilber, Ken, *The Spectrum of Consciousness*. Wheaton, Illinois: Theosophical Publishing House, 1977.

————, *The Atman Project*. Wheaton, Illinois: Theosophical Publishing House, 1980.

————, *No Boundary*. Boulder: Shambhala, 1981.

————, *Up From Eden*. Boulder: Shambhala, 1981.

————, ed., *The Holographic Paradigm and Other Paradoxes*. Boulder & London: Shambhala, New Science Library, 1982.

————, *Eye to Eye: The Quest for the New Paradigm*. Garden City, New York: Anchor Books, 1983.

————, ed., *Quantum Questions: Mystical Writings of the World's Great Physicists*. Boston & London: Shambhala, New Science Library, 1984.

————, Engler, Jack and Brown, Daniel P., *Transformations of Consciousness*. Boston & London: Shambhala, New Science Library, 1986.

Wilson, Larry, *Changing the Game: The New Way to Sell*. New York: Simon & Schuster, 1987.

Woodman, Marion. *From Addiction to Perfection*. Toronto: Inner City Books, 1982.

————, *The Owl Was A Baker's Daughter: Obesity, Anorexia Nervosa and the Repressed Feminine*. Toronto: Inner City Books, 1980.

————, *The Pregnant Virgin: A Process of Psychological Transformation*. Toronto: Inner City Books, 1985.

Young, Arthur M. *The Reflexive Universe: Evolution of Consciousness*. Mill Valley, California: Robert Briggs Associates, 1976.

Zaleznik, Abraham, *The Managerial Mystique: Restoring Leadership in Business*. New York: Harper & Row, 1989.

Zukav, Gary. *The Seat of the Soul*. New York: Simon and Schuster, 1989.

ABOUT CONNEXIONS UNLIMITED...

Connexions Unlimited, Inc., located in Tucson, Arizona, is an educational and service organization dedicated to helping organizations and individuals with transformative change. Initial program offerings, launched in the fall of 1992, will feature a series of workshops presented by nationally known consultants and trainers. The Learning Center programs will emphasize experiences that help businesses integrate profound personal-organizational change, expand creativity and teamwork and undertake substantive renewal efforts.

Connexions Unlimited also has a nonprofit foundation that accepts tax-deductible contributions. The foundation is especially interested in securing funds for "Synthesis Task Force" projects that would bring together leading experts to integrate various aspects of the new organizational paradigm. The task forces would be aided in their work by teams of highly trained facilitators to assure the most efficient process and creative outcomes.

For further information, contact:

Alice Mack, Ed.D., CEO
Connexions Unlimited
7344 North Oracle Road, Suite 194
Tucson, AZ 85704

Connexions Unlimited
6336 N. Oracle Rd. #326-314
Tucson, AZ 85704-5480
http://www.connexionsunltd.com